Poems and Such to Keep in Touch

Elvis "Raz" Stephens

Victoria Fletcher
hootbookspublishing.biz
vfletcher56@gmail.com

Dedication

This poem book is dedicated to people who find humor in life and can also get serious when the situation calls for seriousness.

The poems are designed to make you smile and think and then recall that, "Yes, that is the way it is and the way it was."

These poems are a designated outlet for anyone who wants to read and escape for a few minutes without dedicating an enormous length of time to the book.

Please enjoy and acknowledge that they were written just for your amusement and enjoyment.

This book is dedicated to each of you.

Sincerely,
Elvis "Raz" Stephens

Acknowledgments

Thank you for purchasing this little poem book.

The idea for any and each of the poems came from people who said to write about a particular subject.

Some of the ideas came from the newspaper each day. A lot of the ideas came from the Facebook postings that I read and smiled, laughed, and then thought to use that idea in a poem.

My go-to-guy for assistance and input is my best friend, Dorsey Kimbrell. He often assisted me and made sure I did not get away from the premise of the poem.

The characters in the poems are incidental and if you recognize any of them, be assured they are used for humor and not vilified at all.

A special thank you to my readers.

Each of the 11 books I have done were published by Victoria Fletcher of Hoot Books Publishing. You can find her info on the copyright page in case you want to contact her or have one of your own books published.

Thank each of you so very much.

Table of Contents

Elvis "Raz" Stephens

A Good Day For A Yard Sale

Today's what I call a 'Goldilocks' day
with this warm sunshine so bright
It is not too hot and not too cold
as Goldilocks says, "Just right."

A great day for a huge yard sale.
Lots of stuff put out on display.
Already to go and looking good
for all who will come this way.

Yard selling was a regular thing.
On Saturday, they were all 'round.
People would have to look at it all
to see whatever could be found.

A dollar was a pretty good deal.
You'd stuff your vehicle to the brim.
Mattered not how much or how many,
you would bring home all of them.

It seemed healthy to be out and about.
You knew each street by their name.
If they had them, you sure wanted it.
It was laying there for you to claim.

Then one big day, you would decide
to have your own, since it was so nice.
You'd get rid of all that collected stuff.
You would sell everything for half-price.

A Song In My Heart

Speaking to yourselves in psalms and hymns.
Singing, making a melody in your heart to Him.
What a great way to go along on your way,
saying words that the songwriter did say.

Have you ever heard a song that touched you so
you repeated o'er and o'er wherever you'd go?
You'd find yourself singing it throughout the day.
You'd call the Christian radio and ask them to play.

Music plays an instrumental (little pun there) role
in our hearts and lives and is good for the soul.
We've been given the privilege to lift-up our voice.
We can even whistle or hum as we rejoice.

To worldly songs we give far too much place.
They don't mention Him nor speak of His grace.
We will catch ourselves singing right along
to this ungodly music and this ungodly song.

But today, I am thinking of a great melody.
It encourages and fills me to the full with glee.
I whistle, hum, and sing it right from the start.
It makes me so happy to have a song in my heart.

A Tale of Two Brothers

There were two brothers who ran roughshod
over the town as if they were some kind of god.
They were always mean and inconsiderate, too,
taking advantage of others in all they would do.

They did not care how disadvantaged you were.
They looked for each opportunity to occur
when they could their next swindle do
and then they would pull a 'one-up' on you.

People avoided them as much as they could.
Knowing if they could take you, they surely would.
Seeing either one coming, you'd cross the street.
Not wanting any encounter, perchance to meet.

One day, like wildfire, news in that town spread.
One of those rotten brothers today was now dead.
People had so much that they wanted to say
but they knew there would be repercussions to pay.

The surviving brother wanted to show his respect
so he asked the preacher his brother's good to reflect.
"I'll give you a thousand dollars if you will only tell
that my brother went to heaven instead of to hell."

The preacher had a dilemma about how to share.
How could he tell the people in attendance there?
He said, "Here lies a cheating swindler, weep if you can,
but compared to his brother, he was a good man."

A Tendency To Overanalyze

Dear Abby: The writer begins their inquiry,
I think that I am really quiet the prize.
Yet people do not warm up to me at all.
Could it be that I tend to overanalyze?

I think on things and I understand
why they have to be and go that way.
But then I re-think and change my mind
deciding something different today.

"The best plans of mice and men
so often go awry," I've heard said.
I take that as truth and I believe it.
I cannot settle things in my head.

I have a tendency to sit and think
mulling things over in my mind.
What if I were to do that this way,
could peace and joy I then find?

Life is full of unanswered questions
but I tend to muddle on through.
So, I ask you now, "What do you think?
What is it that I must surely do?"

Maybe yes, then again, maybe no.
Is there something I've failed to realize?
Have I made the best decision I could?
I have a tendency to overanalyze.

A Time For Teaching

Instead of buying for your children
things you were never bought,
try teaching them the things
that you were never taught.

Selfishness is so easily learned.
We form a 'give me' attitude.
Others are then pushed aside
to the point of being rude.

When they show dissatisfaction,
we give in to each little whim.
It seems to be much easier
instead of teaching them.

We're supposed to be the parent,
not their friend with whom they play.
If we let them make the decisions,
we will regret all that one day.

With Christmas coming on so fast,
their wish list will overwhelm.
They'll want this and this and this.
You'll be in another realm.

Teach them that you sincerely care.
That you'll love them no matter what.
Teach them more is not the answer.
Just be thankful for the gifts they got.

Anticipating The Future

"I don't know about tomorrow,
I just live from day to day."
The songwriter told us saying,
"For its skies may turn to grey."

We look forward to our future
anticipating what will happen then.
Those of us who are a Christian
know that we will surely win.

We don't look for the tribulation
that we read and study about.
For we will not even be here
because we have been taken out.

We anticipate the coming rapture
knowing our future is just up ahead.
We anticipate, being ever anxious.
"I'll return for you," Jesus said.

Those left behind had anticipated
somehow, someway, they'd go too.
But the decision needs be made now
or the rapture will not include you.

We anticipate and the church waits
for the future coming of our King.
You can ignore and be left out.
Anticipate the future that will bring.

Are We Desperate Enough?

We often see something we want.
We'll say, "I want that desperately!"
And soon, that will be followed by,
"Man, that means so much to me."

Material things oft strike our fancy.
"I have to have me one of those."
But we seem not to care about
the soul of man and where it goes.

We witness not nor do we tell them
the doom of man who won't believe.
Of the certain everlasting punishment
that all unbelievers will then receive.

We need to be desperate in this matter
warning family who are now lost.
Desperate enough to warn them saying,
"Salvation is free, there is not a cost."

Desperation is very often driven
by what we need to see in others.
As their life to us seems haphazard,
we want them as our sisters, brothers.

To see family and friends struggling,
not knowing Christ makes their life tough.
Let me ask you this important question,
"Are we desperate enough?"

Basic Human Decency

There are a lot of actors in the world
who learn and play a certain role.
And I guess we need to see those.
Some of the better ones touch our soul.

There are those who play their part well.
I couldn't do what they do if I tried.
Others let you know they're not playing.
There is no decency being applied.

Some will step on you and do not care.
They only care for good ole number one.
They will use you and then abuse you.
And cast you away when they are done.

There is no equal or even treatment.
They desire not what is best for you.
This selfish thing done in selfish manner.
It is all for them, this thing they do.

No 'Do unto others as you would have them
do unto you'. They've thrown that out fast.
Sure, you may have done them a favor
but that was way back there in the past.

As a society today, we are very lacking.
Not what I can do for you, but me.
The one thing I would like to see go viral
is the practice of basic human decency.

Be A Beacon

"Let your light so shine before men..." (Matt 5:16)

What does it take for a lighthouse to shine?
How is that related to what we are doing?
It shines out over the troubled waters
giving us light in what we are pursuing.

The church promotes our shining for others.
In times of darkness, we're what they see.
Our circle of friends will oft need our light
to light our neighborhood and community.

Maintenance is important to keep our light
to make sure our lighthouse is in good shape.
A run-down lighthouse is a danger to all.
You would not go to its light for an escape.

You would make sure there's oil in its reservoir.
Older lighthouses made sure to have that on hand.
That, to us, is the Holy Spirit in the forefront
keeping our light burning, helping us to stand.

We do not shine our light just to be viewed.
We're to warn those who'd crash on the reef.
Our light doesn't shine for curious observers.
It shines to guide those growing in their belief.

We're to submit to the Master of the lighthouse.
He evaluates our beacon as it puts forth its shine.
Our beacon-keeper is our biblical authority
keeping our beacons lighted, both yours and mine.

Beatitudes

We look at the beatitudes
as the attitudes to be.
They tell us how to live and
what other folk should see.

Blessed are the poor in spirit.
Theirs is the kingdom on high.
Blessed are they that mourn.
They'll receive comfort and get by.

Blessed are the meek, for they
shall inherit the earth, no less.
Blessed are they which hunger
and thirst after righteousness.

Blessed are the merciful for
mercy they shall obtain.
Blessed are the pure in heart.
They'll see God coming again.

Blessed are the peacemakers,
called children of God they'll be.
Blessed are the persecuted
for their righteousness toward Me.

Blessed are ye when men revile,
falsely all manner of evil they use.
Against you for My sake, I say,
"You'll be rewarded for this abuse."

Being Seen

You see a friend coming
and you give them a smile.
You say, "Long time no see,
haven't seen you in a while."

It's good to have a friendship
and have it often renewed.
I would rather be seen.
It's better than being viewed.

Old friends are a treasure.
We should hold them tight.
It's good to see them often.
They are such a delight.

Being seen is important
we can truly conclude.
It's always better being seen
than it is being viewed.

Berry Pickin' Time

When berries have now ripened
and it's time again to go a pickin',
you will not worry very much
about all the briars a stickin'.

I put on my sticker britches
to wade into the thicket.
I see a huge, juicy berry
and I am gonna pick it.

The biggest and most juicy
were the ones I wanted first,
until my berry bucket
was filled and almost burst.

Berry pickin' time was special.
We each enjoyed it a lot.
We were excited to get back
to see what all we got.

We made sure we had enough
so that they could be canned.
And in the long wintertime,
plenty of berries were on hand.

Cobblers and pies aplenty
from berries picked by each kid.
When it was 'berry pickin' time,
that is what we siblings did.

Bitterness Is Bad

Bitterness is bad, believe it or not,
like a bad apple causing the bushel to rot.
Mercy is the tenderness of the heart we share,
showing to an offender that we still care.

Sometimes we get so angry that we
can't allow ourselves any goodness to see.
We get so mad at what happened before,
we want to go about slamming each door.

Bitterness isn't better. It is a proven fact.
Though it may be the way that we act.
We can huff and puff and carry on mad
but the truth remains, bitterness is bad.

It doesn't take much to cause us to grieve
when we wear our feelings out on our sleeve.
The least little thing will then bring our ire.
Some would then say, "That sets me on fire!"

So, they strike out as mad as can be,
showing no mercy to you nor to me.
Giving no thought to experiences they've had,
nor remembering that bitterness is bad,

We give in to anger and we want all to know,
this is the way things are now going to go,
But I implore you, please do not be mad.
It causes much woe 'cause bitterness is bad.

Carpenter Bees

In the spring, you will see them hovering around.
They do not build nests or burrow into the ground.
They are named for their habit of boring a hole
into softer wood. Making homes is their goal.

They prefer unpainted wood, to them that is fine.
They love redwood, cedar, cypress, and pine.
Pressure treated wood is less likely their delight.
Eaves, rafters, and fascia boards will be the sight.

Their drilling is often evidenced by their muffled hum.
Leaving dust under outdoor furniture, there will be some.
They resemble bumblebees but their tummy is bright.
Bumblebees are more hairy, black and yellow in sight.

Carpenters burrow into wood to lay their eggs there.
They do not have colonies, nor do they even care.
In winter, the adults in their tunnels often remain.
Then in spring they will come crawling out again.

They will fertilize the females who then begin to bore
making a place for their eggs to hatch once more.
The female will lay about six egg cells inside.
They'll be fed by the pollen she leaves to provide.

She fills each chamber with pulp she regurgitates.
Hatching and maturation happens as she waits.
And soon their foraging for flowers has begun.
She will return in the fall for her hibernation.

Come On In (And Rock A While)

We oft find ourselves in such a hurry,
chasing after one more worry.
No time to spend in relaxation.
Dealing with great aggravation.

Always rushing to and fro.
No particular place to go.
Just spinning like a twirling top.
Seemingly, we never stop.

Seems only a few years ago,
people were not rushing so.
They'd take time to sit a bit
but we've lost the hang of it.

Much time spent in this and that,
nervous as a two-tailed cat.
Darting 'round all o'er the place,
way too busy is our case.

Stores used to have rockers where
even active people often sat
saying in their inviting style,
"Come on in and rock a while."

Porches had them in a line.
When we sat, soon all was fine.
Rocking brings a restful smile.
Just come on in and rock a while.

Common Sense and Logic

If you will but look and listen,
you'll soon realize very fast
that common sense and logic
have become things of the past.

Our thinking is no longer logical.
Common sense has left the scene.
We want to make good decisions
and live a life that is serene.

We have become so complacent.
Outside influence has come to bare
to fill the void that now exists with
common sense and logic no longer there.

We oft scratch our heads and wonder,
What in the world is going on?
We can't agree on important issues
and we get left out there all alone.

We are confused and misdirected.
Common sense and logic are gone today.
It does not seem to take much notice
because we weren't using them anyway.

Confusion, Cares and Concerns

Does anything take a believer by surprise
about anything going on in the world out there:
the international conflicts, government corruption,
the ecclesiastic confusion, and our personal care?

We could extend this list almost to ad infinitum
yet the believer has reason to maintain great hope.
We can be joyful because of certain verities.
With God still in control, we can assuredly cope.

God has His proverbial eye on each one of us.
Though so often we struggle and find the way hard,
He works all things to the counsel of His own will.
We learn that nothing will catch God off guard.

An entire volume could be written about
the supernal blessings that are promised us here.
And we are blessed with all spiritual blessings
to be enjoyed now and the time coming near.

As we seek comfort, contentment, and courage
here in the twenty-first century's volatile days,
the confusion, cares, and concerns we're facing
will be addressed by God in some miraculous ways.

"Yea, I have loved thee with an everlasting love.
Therefore, with loving kindness have I drawn thee."
God's loving concern is for all who will believe.
There's never a time when His hand we can't see.

Consider Yourself Fortunate

If you cannot understand why someone
is still grieving for so very long,
consider yourself fortunate that you
to this group you do not belong.

If you have never known great hunger,
you've always had something to eat,
consider yourself fortunate that you
have never begged out on the street.

If you've never been chilled by the cold
but have always seemed to be inside,
consider yourself very fortunate
that the Lord did for you provide.

If you have never searched for one
to extend to you their open hand,
consider yourself fortunate that
you haven't had to understand.

God provides for those who love Him.
He takes care of those who trust.
He tells us let things go so we can
see how good He is to all of us.

We are fortunate beyond all measure.
His blessings He will freely bestow.
If you will consider yourself fortunate,
His blessings then will overflow.

Control-Alt-Delete

You started out strong but was soon defeated
as if someone had control-alt-deleted.
You now just sit there and stare at length.
Something has zapped all of your strength.

If you get hung up as you go your way,
it is refreshing to oft stop and pray.
It may take a while to get things completed.
Just make sure you are not control-alt-deleted.

To control-alt-delete the mess we are in
allows us to then start all over again.
When in some situations this would be ideal,
we could clean the slate and keep it real.

We begin okay, our plan is well laid out.
Chin up, eyes forward as we go about.
But little mishaps pop up, not so endearing.
We wipe them away with three keys clearing.

This idea is true in whatever the case.
In all of the things we need to erase.
Being able to start over makes life complete.
Thank God He gives us His control-alt-delete.

Cutting Wood Is Good

The sun is shining and it is nice and warm.
I am so glad to have a day like today.
The house gets chilly without any heat
but a warm fire will chase the cold away.

I usually have a sizeable stack of wood
chopped and ready to be hauled in.
I load it into the wheelbarrow often
and roll it up to the house once again.

Sawing and chopping, and piling it up
makes me feel exceptionally good.
Even in the cold, I sweat just a little.
No better exercise than working in wood.

Using my muscles to split each chunk.
Using axe or maul, whichever I desire.
It is what each piece will offer me
when I put it into the warming fire.

The crackle of wood as it burns
allows me to just sit back and smile.
I get the enjoyment of being warm
as each piece will last for a little while.

Did I tell you I think it is healthy?
I think others would do it if they could.
I am convinced that it helps me much.
I believe that cutting wood is good.

Deliverance From Entrapment   (Exodus 14)

(Derived from Pastor Brandon Haskett's Sunday night message at CBC 12-26-21)

Israel had been in Egypt for many long years as we know
when God spoke to Moses. It was time for them to go.
They exited the city and soon were entrapped by the sea.
They were entangled in the land, shut in tight as could be.

God said, "I will now harden Pharaoh's wicked heart
and all of his host in Egypt that shall take his part
that I shall have honor of king Pharaoh and his host.
They shall know I am the Lord, the one they fear the most."

The king gathered up his chariots and all of his horsemen
and they chased after Israel to bring them back again.
Pursuing and overtaking them was the plan Pharaoh made.
With Egyptians marching after them, they were sore afraid.

They cried out unto the Lord and to Moses they began to say,
"There were no graves in Egypt, why hast thou taken us away?
Moses said, "Fear not, stand still, His salvation He'll release.
"The Lord shall fight for you and ye shall hold your peace."

The angel of God that was leading them moves to the behind
and separates the two so that the one cannot the other find.
A strong east wind blew all night and in the morning it was found,
God's children went into the midst of the sea upon dry ground.

The chariots and Pharaoh's horsemen followed them to a man.
The waters closed upon them, the wheels came off his plan.
Then Israel saw the Egyptians lying dead upon the shore.
They were not entangled nor entrapped by Pharaoh any more.

Distractions Come So Easily

My intentions were of the highest regard.
Doing that thing was not so very hard.
I was ready to go to the extra mile
but I got distracted for a little while.

I wanted to get back to it in a hurry.
It was causing me somewhat to worry.
But the time just never did seem right
so, I'll give it some time and then I might.

Why do my plans so often go awry?
I fully understand the what and why.
But soon distractions take me away
with thoughts of completing it one day.

Distractions come and get in between
the start and the ending that is seen.
So, I don't finish the things I deem.
Distractions come so easily it seems.

Do you likewise have things to adhere
And distractions come to interfere.
You prefer to stay on a steady pace.
Soon distractions you will have to face.

When that happens yet again to me,
I try to accept them because you see
I had planned for them there to be
because distractions come so easily.

Do Your Very Best

I have learned a little something
that helps me pass each test.
Get in church and stay in church
and do your very best.

Times are tough for each of us
and at times we all will struggle.
A lot of things come into play
that are so difficult to juggle.

But if we do our very best
and depend on His assistance,
He will help us on our way
to overcome each resistance.

"Do your very best," they say,
offering encouragement to us.
They know we will need that
and His Spirit will renew us.

We wake up, do our daily prayer,
then begin our work anew.
We must take Jesus with us.
He assists us in what to do.

I would say this is a challenge
but yet it gives us peace and rest.
Just step out, go forth, and conquer
and each day do your very best.

Doesn't Matter

There is a new thing going around today
that people often are heard to say.
Maybe they are beginning to lose touch.
It seems that it "doesn't matter" much.

"Antimatter" comes from cosmic rays
but we don't worry about that these days.
We lay around getting fatter and fatter.
Stuff like that just "doesn't matter".

"Dark matter" is out there in our universe.
If we didn't have it, things would be worse.
It's the remnants of large stars now dead.
We've better things to worry about instead.

Our life here on earth is to be enjoyed
instead of useless things our mind employed.
We can allow ourselves to be much sadder.
Just worrying 'bout what "doesn't matter".

Eagles Fly Alone

Ofttimes, you may seem outnumbered
in the thing you wish to do.
Others seem not to even care about
what is important now to you.

They will say, "You don't need that,
you're wasting your time," they'll say.
But if they could see it as you see it,
then everything would be okay.

You are flying high and looking low.
You see what others cannot see.
They are satisfied with status quo.
More than willing to let things be.

Don't stir the pot, don't make a fuss.
Just go along with what's in place.
If you mess up the accepted practice,
you will have egg upon your face.

Let me encourage you in your doings.
Fly high and soar o'er all the nays.
Stay above all the mixed confusion.
You will be happier in all your days.

Don't be afraid of being outnumbered.
The pigeon flock will soon be gone.
Stand up, step out, and be counted.
It is a proven fact eagles fly alone.

Either, Neither, Nor

These words are sometimes interchanged,
although they are somewhat each correct.
But it does matter how you use them.
Maybe they are used just for the effect.

"Either" is used before the first of two
or occasionally more alternatives specified.
The other being introduced by "or".
"Either" I'll go with you, "or" I'll abide.

"Neither" is used often to indicate
you have decided between at least two
alternatives that are being specified.
That "neither" one is considered as true.

It is used to indicate that each is untrue.
Of things being considered, it is "neither".
We must be careful not to misstate it.
It is not one or the other, not either.

"Nor" is just a little trickier in its use.
It is used before the second alternative
being specified and introduced by "nor"
to get the attention it needs to receive.

It says other considerations are not true.
That it can't be "nor" was it infused.
They can be confusing as we use them.
When "either", "neither", and nor is used.

English 101 Requirement

My English professor in college would say,
"If you are late for class, you will have to pay.
You must write a verse about the why
or at least give it your very best try."

One day for class, I was running behind.
I needed to hurry so as not to find
that an example to others I would soon be,
having to write a verse just wasn't for me.

As I came across the parking lot, I could see
a big bull-dozer pushing on a huge tree.
The aim was to remove it, take it away.
The parking lot was to be paved today.

I got intrigued and decided to stay
until that huge tree on the ground did lay.
He would push on one side, making it unstable,
then push the other as much as able.

Back and forth, on and on, doing this event,
I forgot about the time that was being spent.
I hastened off to class, running on the double,
I'd have to write a verse, knowing I was in trouble.

This is my verse:
There she stood since her birth
planted firmly in Mother Earth.
She was up-rooted on this date.
I saw it all, that's why I was late.

Expectations

Boast not thyself of tomorrow because
you know not what the new day will bring.
It could be filled with good expectations
or have much sadness and sorrowing.

Life is filled with the good and bad.
We know not which way it will come.
It may or may not be as expected.
It will mean different things for some.

Perhaps we expect a certain thing
to happen in a time and place.
Then we're utterly overwhelmed
with disappointment on our face.

When something good has happened,
we want others to hear it fast
or it could be the worst of news.
We want assurance it will not last.

Each day we take on obligations
and expect that all we will achieve.
We strive to make them a reality
expecting many blessings to receive.

Paul warns us to not be unsettled,
to have peace in all of our ways,
to put on meekness and kindness
expecting God's blessing all our days.

Famous Atheists' Last Words

"Only fools say in their hearts, there is no God." (Psalm 14:1)

When Gandhi lay there upon his death bed,
these are the recorded words that he said,
"I find myself in slough and despond."
He is beginning to see what lies beyond.

"All about me is darkness," he said in fright.
Then he concluded, "I am praying for light."
Great as Gandhi was, this was his last breath,
and soon his life had been swallowed in death.

Sir Thomas Scott, at the time of his death did tell,
"I thought there was neither God nor hell.
Now I know there are both," and I trust,
"I am doomed to perdition by the Just."

Thomas Payne, American writer now long gone
begged, "Stay with me, please don't leave me alone."
"O God help me, I long for your touch.
What have I done to suffer so much?"

"What will become of me hereafter?" he pled.
"I would give worlds, if I had them," he said.
"That The Age of Reasoning had never been written.
O Lord, help me, Christ, help me, I am now smitten."

"No, don't leave; stay with me! Do not be gone.
I am on the edge of hell as I lie here all alone.
Send even a child that would hold my hand.
I've been the devils' agent," too late I understand.

Feel, Felt, Found

People ask me, "How do you feel?"
And then they will ask my age.
I feel the way I've always felt.
I'm still on the very same page.

I always feel the way I always felt
unless a better way I have found.
Then, of course, people will say,
"What goes around comes around."

In my heart I am still a little boy
with all the health, vim, and vigor.
I really haven't aged that much
though I've gotten somewhat bigger.

Decisions are made by what we feel
and by how we have felt in the past.
Then later a much better way is found.
Then the first decision will not last.

OR, we have time to rethink it all
deciding we were right from the start.
We still feel now as we felt then.
We have found that is our heart.

Being older hopefully means wiser.
We will take a stand on solid ground.
We're not too old to share things.
How we feel, we felt, then we found.

Flamingo Mothers

When you think of flamingo mothers
and how they spend their days,
they will remind us of ourselves
in a lot of different ways.

They will wade out into life
and make us overly proud.
As they take on various challenges
standing out in any crowd.

They spend time with their flock,
glad to have others around.
Always finding the right balance.
Making sure happiness is found.

They are flexible in their doings
and will keep their beaks all clean.
They're not afraid to get their feet wet.
No ruffled feathers will be seen.

Mothers are special where e'er you see them.
They are flexible and fabulous too.
They take their stand as the flamingo.
Mothers know what's best to do.

Forgiving One Another

We are not to grieve the Holy Spirit of God
with the bitterness and wrath we do every day.
Our anger, clamor, and our evil-speaking,
along with all malice are to be put away.

We are to be tenderhearted and forgiving
even as Christ has forgiven both you and me.
God, for Christ's sake, forgave each and all.
This fact is well known, given to us free.

"The first shall be last" is an attitude
that we put into action in all our doing.
It should be at the very top of all we do
as we go forth along our way pursuing.

An unforgiving spirit causes God much grief.
It is close to ingratitude in our mind.
As we think not upon the past events
when His forgiveness we did quickly find.

Tenderhearted and being kind are twins.
They each grow from the very same place.
Both enrooted from our hearts' attitude.
Walking hand-in-hand in God's garden of grace.

Bitterness, wrath, anger, and evil-speaking
should end up on the Christian's trash heap.
We should practice forgiving one another
making sure none of these things we keep.

Elvis "Raz" Stephens

Fox In The Henhouse

'Fox in the henhouse' can mean many things.
It usually means that something went wrong.
The result was something completely different.
Things were turned upside down before long.

We had all our eggs in one basket and then
something unexpectedly ruined the entire lot.
We had hoped for the best but, nonetheless,
the result was certainly not what we got.

If we had to describe our disappointment
as to how things had gone so much awry,
the answer would come to us very quickly.
The proverbial 'fox in the henhouse' is why.

The fox sneaks in when least expected.
He will do his damage and will then run.
Being on our toes and on our vigil will not
always prevent the damage that is done.

He just may be a tiny little creature
that will pop up his sly little head.
You think all is covered, but you find
that 'fox in the henhouse' instead.

Make sure you know what is happening.
Do not let intrusion happen to you.
The open entry will soon be discovered.
Because that is what foxes always do.

Freedom Or Loneliness?

When nobody wakes you up in the morning,
and when nobody waits for you at night,
and when you can do whatever you want,
does that make you feel everything's alright?

When you can go as you want, do as you please
as if you have not even one little care.
Do you enjoy it as much as you could
having no one to go with you to share?

Do you champion the time you are alone.
The stillness and quietness that can be found.
Do you even seek companionship of others
and enjoy having many people around.

You can be alone and yet not be lonely
and yet the opposite is certainly true.
There can be lots of people there with you
and yet deep loneliness soon will ensue.

They say loneliness is not a physical condition.
We look at it as being a state of mind.
Losing someone we love can be heart wrenching.
Then a great loneliness is left there behind.

Maybe it just depends upon your perception:
The who, what, when and so I ask you,
to your own self, now try to be honest,
freedom or loneliness, which is your view?

Gas and Gospel Shortage

We're so worried about having gasoline.
Not being able to get from here to there.
Yet when it comes to sharing the gospel,
we have not the mind to give it care.

The shortage of gas is much talked about.
We are reminded each day in the news.
But sharing the good news of the gospel
is an opportunity that we seldom use.

I heard the newsman say last night,
"There is plenty enough gasoline
but getting it where it needs to go,
distribution is the lack we've seen."

My mind immediately saw a parallel
between gas and the gospel thus,
there will always be a shortage when
the distribution depends upon us.

Jesus told us that we are to go
into the world and the gospel teach.
Regardless of how much gas there is,
there are yet people we can reach.

You may not believe there is a shortage.
The first one may depend on how you feel.
That's okay, but let me assure you
that the second one is very real.

Give It All You Got

Some people do things piecemeal,
not putting their heart into it.
When it's finished, it'll be okay.
They think that's the way to do it.

No effort extended nor applied,
just going along to get it done.
Being careless in the completion.
Having to finish it on the run.

You decide it's okay to postpone.
There is no need to even worry.
And if the time then becomes late,
you can accomplish it in a hurry.

Dragging your feet is not the best
because time cannot be extended.
It is always better to get it done
before the given time has ended.

Getting totally involved early on
brings a better outcome more than not.
Success is measured by involvement.
Get in there and give it all you got.

Give Today A Chance

Today is a day that the Lord has made.
Let us be glad and rejoice in it.
And when that struggle comes against us,
I am sure that we can win it.

If we but give today a chance,
it will show itself to be great.
It will bring forth a certain blessing
just when you thought it too late.

The day may start off with darkness
but the sun will come shining through.
If we but give today a chance,
what wonders our God will then do.

God says we have not because we ask not.
So we ought to make sure that we ask.
Because He has already assured us,
in today's goodness we can bask.

They say opportunities are a dime a dozen.
I doubt seriously if that is true.
But I do believe if you give today a chance,
you will find happiness and life anew.

And so my friend, you get to decide
which road you are going to travel.
Are you willing to give today a chance?
God's love and mercy He will unravel.

God Also Chose Joseph

We know full well the story of Mary.
How God chose her above the rest.
Of all women living in the world,
it was she who would be the best.

We tend to overlook her husband,
betrothed to her though yet unwed.
Joseph was of the lineage of David.
The angel appeared unto him and said,

"Do not fear to take unto thee Mary
for she is conceived of the Holy Ghost."
And Joseph proved to be the just man
that Father God had aforetime chose.

Joseph would offer the child protection
against the evil that King Herod devised.
He took his family and fled into Egypt
as the angel of the Lord that night advised.

Later when King Herod was then dead,
the angel told Joseph to take his wife
and young child with him, going in peace.
They're dead who sought the young child's life.

Joseph proved to be totally yielded
and obedient to all within God's plan.
He was selfless in all of his doings
as the earthly father of the God Man.

Going Along With The Herd

Going along to get along is not always true.
Try it if you want but it may not be good for you.
Some of the things that others carry out
just may leave you with some serious doubt.

They may coerce you to join right in,
"It'll make you happier than you've ever been."
But you know right from the very start
that it is not what is in your heart.

They are your friends and so you may abide
saying, "I'm just going along for the ride."
But later you wish you had not done that.
Trying to be accepted is not where it is at.

Hopefully you have your very own mind
and will decide not to do things of that kind.
You will stay above the turmoil and fray.
You know things aren't to happen that way.

Have a good reputation, doing what is correct,
then one day you can look back and reflect
that when they cried for something so loud,
you stood up to stand out in the misguided crowd.

Please let me encourage you to be your own.
You will be glad of it once you are grown.
Stay positive in action, in deed, and in word.
You'll get nowhere going along with the herd.

Going Tradin'

I think today is going to be that day
when I go tradin' and have to pay
to get some groceries I need to eat:
some things needful, some just sweet.

Older folks used to call it that name,
Going Tradin' when that day came.
Today we get staples that we need.
It is time to do that dreadful deed.

Toiletries, hand towels all thrown in,
with canned goods ready in the tin,
milk and bread are the main things,
with side items that necessity brings.

Tradin' was a huge deal years ago.
You only went once a month or so.
You only bought some necessary stuff
cause times then were ordinarily tough.

But today people seem to enjoy it.
Going tradin' every chance they get.
It was once a labor to go to the store
up out of the holler to go for more.

We raised most of our food alone.
Went to the store when it was gone.
But today, going tradin' is not a chore.
People seem to enjoy going to the store.

Gone With The Wind

The wind seems to come from nowhere
and it moves things around when it blows.
It can be both your friend, or maybe not,
and dangerous too, as everyone knows.

It can turn things over or upside down
and spill stuff that you wanted to keep.
Make a huge mess in its boisterous wake
leaving stuff amok in a piled-up heap.

Then again, it can be a little helpful.
It'll blow the leaves right out of your yard.
You will not have to even rake them.
That way you will not be too tired.

The limbs from the trees will soon fall.
You will then have to attend to those.
Break them up into the garbage can.
They'll disappear when the garbage goes.

The flag will need to be properly tied
or else it will become ragged and torn,
pulled out of the grommets that hold it
and away in the wind it'll be born.

Wouldn't it be nice if our problems
could be cast into it and carried away.
We could be rid of them forever and
they would be gone with the wind today.

Half Full or Half Empty

When talking about your blessings,
someone just may use this phrase,
they say, "My cup is either half full
or half empty on most days."

I think we are truly blessed
and we see that every day.
Some may not be in agreement.
They just waste their time away.

But I tend to look at my cup
and I know it has over-flowed.
And by the Lord's good graces,
I keep on going down my road.

So go ahead now and ask me,
"Is my cup half full or half empty?"
I just may answer, "It is both.
Just to have one makes me happy."

That saying is supposed to be funny,
being a half-full or half empty cup.
Either way I receive His blessings.
I praise the Lord He fills mine up.

Handfuls of Purpose

When Ruth went out into the field that day
to gather grain that fell by the way,
the master of the field came by and said,
"Leave handfuls of purpose for her bread."

His kindness exceeded any she had seen
allowing her with the reapers to glean.
She knew that she had truly been blessed
by the handfuls of purpose for her they left.

There were thousands of men on the hillside that day.
One of the disciples said, "Send them away.
This is a desert place and the time is now past.
There is no way to feed a number this vast."

But Jesus said, "They are to depart not.
Give them to eat of what we have got."
So, with five loaves and two fishes their hunger was met.
Twelve baskets of handfuls of purpose were gathered up yet.

Jesus said to forgive and ye shall forgiven be.
If we give only to receive, what thanks have we?
"Give and it shall be given to you once more.
Good measure, pressed down, shaken together, running o'er."

"The same measure that you measure out to and man
shall be measured out unto you once again."
For man's body and his soul cannot contain
God's handfuls of purpose that will yet remain.

He Already Knows

So many difficulties we each must go through
when we have no idea what we must then do.
We go stumbling along as we worry and we fret.
All because we have not considered Him as yet.

We use what little strength we have to carry on,
until all of our energy is depleted and now gone.
Then we sit and we wonder as to the reason why.
Maybe it is now time to give God a try.

He could have already intervened in the mix.
And to our satisfaction brought about the fix.
We hesitate to tell Him and the problem grows.
It will not surprise Him, He already knows.

He knows all about what we need to ask.
How we've failed to measure up to the task.
He is ever ready but will with patience wait
for us to let it go and no longer hesitate.

The answer's waiting there just out of our sight,
but we must search for it in the proper light.
We learn it has already been for us revealed.
It is not now hidden and it is not concealed.

He loves when we ask and seek Him and thus,
He has the answer ready and freely gives to us.
Let us trust and tell Him about all of our woes.
Why keep them from Him? He already knows.

His Wake-Up List

Sometimes we forget to be thankful
and we just let things be as they are.
We don't put a lot into their happening,
not expecting them to go very far.

We do not always have things planned.
Sometimes we just accept them and say,
"Wow! That was very interesting and yet,
we are glad they turned out that way."

We can be in the right place they say
and at just the right time to be there.
Good things will happen without warning.
We did not even have to prepare.

Our thanks are so often short lived.
Kind of in one ear and out the other.
We do not expect much to be done
from one we call sister or brother.

So, we don't give acknowledgment to them.
Not saying, "You have our thanks for that."
We all know we need be more thankful
but today, it is where our society is at.

God said in all things we're to be thankful.
For everything in our life that doth exist.
The thing I'm ever so thankful for today
is that my name was on His wake-up list.

How To Be Happy

Sometimes being happy is very easy.
Other times it seems so hard to do.
What enlightens and brightens me
just may not be the same for you.

Try turning negatives into positives
and do that which seemeth good.
Not letting small stuff bother you.
Let that all pass by you as you should.

Don't let anyone steal your joy
because true joy is hard to find.
Let all things bring you amusement
to take the cares out of your mind.

Stay away from drama please.
You do not always have to act.
Just face whatever is happening
and deal directly with each fact.

Love and accept yourself always.
Follow the leading of your heart.
If you keep things plain and simple,
you will be happy from the start.

Cherish loved ones, let them know
that on each other you do depend.
No matter what, just be yourself,
that is how to be happy friend.

Elvis "Raz" Stephens

I Am Confused

I do my best to use the proper word
and yet I find it was not correct.
How two words basically are the same
causes me now to stop and reflect.

I am quite, <u>quiet</u> sure I knew which
when I wrote it in my poem's line.
That it went they're and their,
it would be correct and just fine.

But when I re-read it, I then noticed
that it had not been correctly used.
I try to keep my usage <u>rilly</u>, real
but at times I sheerly get confused.

I work hard on using me and I
and can now use them and get <u>bye</u>.
Other words that sound so much alike
cause me pause when I even try.

I think you may yet get my meaning.
Properly or improperly used before.
I did not want to waist the thought.
I am confused and maybe use it <u>pour</u>.

When I <u>misteakingly</u> misspell a word
and use one meaning different instead,
it is not because I do not even <u>no</u>, <u>know</u>
<u>its</u> because I am confused in my head.

I Am Counting

We are often told we do not count.
That's exactly how we're treated today.
But that is not my opinion at all.
I think we all count in our own way.

We take time to count our money.
We use that when we have our fun.
We often count on having more time.
Counting on getting things done.

We count our pounds religiously
making sure we've not gained a bit.
We are fearful that if we do that,
our clothes surely would not fit.

The calories are something we note.
We count them so as not to add more.
Just the amount we allow ourselves,
paying attention to not go o'er.

Counting our steps, writing them down,
bragging to others, the total we tell.
We want all to know how we're doing.
We count on them to wish us well.

I can waste time with all this counting
until it builds and overflows my head.
But that's not for me any longer,
I am counting my blessings instead.

Elvis "Raz" Stephens

I Can't Whistle

Back when people would whistle a lot,
I would try to do what they would.
But I must confess that somehow,
I just was not ever any good.

Knowing the tune did not help.
It still did not come out well.
A few people would encourage me
Saying, "It's as easy as ringing a bell."

But try as I could, I just couldn't.
My lips would not form for the blow.
Such awful noise I would make,
they'd point far away and say, "GO."

Whistling is an art, I believe,
and some people do it with ease.
But when I start whistling for them,
they generally say, "Oh please!"

I reckon I'll stick to humming.
At least I can still carry a tune.
They haven't asked me to stop doing that.
But they probably will pretty soon.

Maybe with a little more practice,
I could catch on and do very well.
For now, they don't want to hear me,
and they have no problem to tell.

I Don't Really Have a Plan

We all know that things work better
when we follow the right plan.
But so often we just hit and miss
and do the very best we can.

We can't see the ending plainly
nor where we are along the way.
We just struggle blindly onward
hoping we'll get here one day.

We aren't aware we are misguided.
We strike out and soon become lost,
becoming overwhelmed by doing.
We haven't tallied up the cost.

People ask us how we're doing
as we struggle along on our way.
We respond weakly in our answer.
We're just too embarrassed to say.

It would've been better, as we know,
had we been much more prepared
for this endeavor we are trying.
Much more time we should've spared.

I have stalled and I've stumbled.
Thought I was doing the best I can.
So now I might as well confess it
because I don't really have a plan.

Elvis "Raz" Stephens

I Plumb Do Not Know

In years past, I thought I knew
about how to do, where to go.
But now I get perplexed
because I plumb do not know.

You think, that's way too easy.
Why does he even fret?
I do not know the answer.
It is not that I forget.

I try to stay balanced,
knowing the things essential.
I daily make a little progress,
Yet, maybe, I am just mental.

If I ask you a question,
please be extra kind.
I just cannot bring things
into my little mind.

Pondering and wondering
will sometimes do the trick.
Other times I just worry
until it makes me quite sick.

Why do I even consider?
Is it yes or is it no?
The correct answer is that
I plumb do not know.

I'd Like To Tell You

I'd like to tell you the world is getting better
but I hope you know that is not true.
According to the Bible, it's going to get worse
and the Bible tells us all what we must do.

If we do not yet today know of Jesus,
it is not too late for those who will believe
and trust Him for the salvation He offers
to us freely, if we will only but receive.

There will come a time when it is too late.
We will wish then we had taken care
and listened to the many warnings
from the ones who took the time to share.

They told us that the good Lord loves us
and that He has gone to prepare a place.
If we had only taken the time to listen,
we could stand unashamed before His face.

I would like to tell you of another option.
If there were one, I'd surely let you know.
But Jesus said that He's the One and only
way to heaven prepared for all of us to go.

To all those alive today who have not decided
to give in and let Jesus have His way,
or from heaven you will be excluded.
Oh, the mourning of regret on that day.

If...

If I'm sitting in my recliner,
doing basketball on my TV.
Please do not give me a call
to interrupt and bother me.

If I'm getting ready to eat
and have just sat at the table,
don't expect me to come running.
for sure then, I'll not be able.

If I am outside doing yardwork
and you need a helping hand,
I must refuse to leave that work.
I ask you to please understand.

If I am listening to my music,
there's no need you drop a dime.
You could come and also listen.
We could have a great ole time.

If I should die before you do,
never again you'll see my face.
Bury with me all my LP records.
It'll be my vinyl resting place.

If I Could Be a Cat

On days when I'm overwhelmed
with worry about this and that,
it's those times I stop and ponder
what it would be like to be a cat.

I could lay there in the window
and watch the squirrels in a tree
instead of having human problems
about what my next meal will be.

Knowing my humans will soon feed me
with delicious morsels as my treat.
They'd load me down with the goodies
knowing the things I love to eat.

I love to be petted and hugged,
Sometimes squeezed really tight.
Knowing I am appreciated much.
Being held when it is night, night.

If being lazy gets the job done,
then I'd be the best at doing that.
My family would be so proud of me.
All things considered, I'd be a cat.

Elvis "Raz" Stephens

If I Only Could

Time is so often fleeting
but there is no repeating.
I can't go back and change
nor can I ever rearrange.

I gave it my best shot,
tho' I missed it by a lot.
Now I must continue on
letting bygones be gone.

We only get one chance.
Do the deed, enjoy the dance.
It'll be over 'fore we know it.
Our life will have to show it.

If we know this going in,
we'll have a chance to win
and possibly accomplish much,
even have the 'golden touch'.

Everything may turn out great.
For some it will not be too late.
Staying positive day after day
will surely go a long, long way.

If you live a lifetime of regret
and have not arrived as of yet,
trust things will turn out good.
Not have to say, "If I only could."

If Only I Had Known

If I had known then what I know now,
things would be different somehow.
No working my fingers to the bone.
Would've known better what's going on.

I could have taken a more steady pace
and not been in the ole rat race.
Could have used my brain, not my brawn,
been more in tune with what's going on.

A busy body doesn't mean success.
Should have taken a scheduled recess.
Relaxed and thought about what I'm doing.
As the many, many things I was pursuing.

If I had known a much better way
to get things done from day to day,
I would not have had to work so hard,
always coming home so very tired.

I had places to go and people to see.
Knowing that they meant a lot to me.
They always came first so on and on.
Could have slowed down if I had known.

Being and doing is not where it's at.
There is much more to life than that.
Soon your kids will be grown and gone.
Now hindsight says, if only I had known.

If The "What Ifs" Were Gone

Lord, You know what I am worried about.
I can't stop thinking about what's next.
I am stressed, unsettled, and so worried,
and all that keeps me much perplexed.

Lord, please take control of my situation.
Strengthen me and guide me day by day.
Help me to focus on the here and now
and please take the "what ifs" away.

Please give me of Your wisdom, Lord.
Help me know what I am to do.
I want Your complete assurance.
In all things, I must trust in you.

My indecision often costs me dearly.
I cannot rightly make up my mind.
I drift in and out of having blessings.
It is Your peace I want to find.

So, I now ask You to kindly show me
what I can accomplish in my heart.
What I can conquer if I but go forth
if those "what ifs" were not a part.

You said we have not because we ask not
so, I am asking You right here and now,
"Please take away all of the 'what ifs
so to Your perfect will, I can now bow.

If We Could

Happiness comes to us in a lot of ways
as we go forth to spend our days.
Some things we'd change from bad to good
and do them all over if we could.

If we could just smile more in fact,
we'd be happier with each contact
with other people we meet no doubt
as we hasten and scurry about.

If we could pay more attention to others,
those who are our Christian brothers,
we could show them they're not alone.
Opportunities like this so soon are gone.

If we could be in it trying to win it
instead of always being "agin" it,
we'd accomplish much more tis true.
Be a better person both me and you.

If we could, we'd do much better
following after Jesus to the letter.
But we give up and shake our head,
happy just being unhappy instead.

If we could lose our salvation, we would.
But we are not saved by all our good.
It's not by works, that's understood.
We would be lost forever if we could.

If You Are Afraid

If you're scared, then say you're scared
or admit that you are sore afraid.
You can't share the good news you know,
to talk of that you'd be dismayed,

You are glad that you heard the gospel.
You are glad it came to you.
But to share that same good news
is something you just cannot do.

I want the preacher and the deacons
to go forth and others tell.
But I am too afraid to try that.
Hopefully, they'll be saved from hell.

I have family and friends, so many
whom I am not sure about.
If they are in the heavenly number,
or are they standing on the out.

Jesus said that we are to "Fear not."
So many things that doth portray.
Basically, it means don't be afraid.
He will give you the words to say.

If you're afraid, you have but to ask.
He will give you what you need.
They want and need to hear the gospel.
Do not be afraid to intercede

I'm A Multi-tasker

I try hard to stay busy each day.
It helps to pass the time away.
Looking for something I can do
to last me for an hour or two.

I think that I'm a multi-tasker.
If I am idle, I have but to ask her
and the wife gives me stuff to do
that'll keep me busy for a few.

Being ambidextrous is so grand,
working well with either hand
gets the job done in a fast hurry.
Not that my time is of a worry.

I am retired and could just sit.
Stuff has something wrong with it.
So I jump in without even asking
and find myself multi-tasking.

If staying busy will get it done,
you'll find me always on the run.
Odd jobs to do and I'm up to it.
Multi-tasking is the way I do it.

Elvis "Raz" Stephens

In Honor of My Friend, Ron Hill

Ron often came by my house
and we would sit for a spell.
I mostly just sat and listened.
He had great stories to tell.

He was constantly staying busy
with many irons in the fire.
People to see, and places to go,
doing for others was his desire.

He was known and liked by many.
I counted Ron as a dear friend.
He went to heaven this morning.
But his story does not now end.

He was a big man in his stature.
He was even bigger in his heart.
We love you, Ron, and we miss you.
Your memory will not depart.

You were a man among men for sure.
Your shoes no one can now fill.
As you reap your reward in heaven,
I will miss my good friend, Ron Hill.

Indelible Imprints

When someone passes away, we so often find
the indelible imprints that they leave behind.
Those indelible imprints are imbedded deep
and they are something that we want to keep.

The way they handled everything they faced
will now be difficult for us to be replaced.
Oh, how precious was the time we spent.
But, we still have their indelible imprint.t

The things they taught us were well received
about whom and what could be believed.
The example set took away all of our doubt
leaving us the wisdom to figure it all out.

Footprints that were imprinted along the way
are going to once again come into play.
Those memories are indelible to us still.
Remembering them today and always will.

This gives us hope that we will be the same.
That people will always want to hear our name.
As is told, the good things we did while here.
Those indelible imprints held so ever dear.

Just know that you are not in this world alone.
You will be remembered long after you are gone.
Let the imprints of your footprints then provide
so that your indelible imprints cannot be denied.

Israel's Arrogant Sinfulness   (Micah 6:9-16)

The merchants used their practice of scant measure
to cheat the common man, building their own treasure.
Then the common man would cheat the poor in return.
God would punish their abominableness as we learn.

They would use wicked balances with a deceitful weight.
The rich were full of violence, God would not hesitate.
God said you have spoken lies and now you all must pay.
Their tongues were deceitful in their mouths all the day.

"Therefore, also will I make thee sick in smiting thee,
in making thee desolate because of thy sins toward Me."
"Thou shalt eat but not be satisfied." Hungry they'd go
as if their stomachs were now empty and they'd know.

"You will have harvested your crops," says the Lord.
But all you've reaped will be taken away by the sword."
The invasion will take away all that you then own.
There will be nothing left because all of it is gone.

"Thou shalt sow, but thou shall not reap," as if you can't.
"Thou shalt tread the olives but the oil will be scant."
He said there will be many grapes upon the vine
but thou shalt not taste nor drink any of the wine.

Israel's people had degenerated to the lowest level
and were now worshipping Omri, follower of the devil.
God is disgusted with the satanic delusion they are in
and He will make them desolate for their awful sin.

It Is Strange

It is strange when twenty dollars seems like a lot
when you take it away from the money you got
and put it into the offering plate as a donation
instead of giving it freely, it is like a violation.

It's strange how two hours is a long time spent
at church listening to preaching, "You must repent!"
When a two-hour movie causes you no fret.
You watch without asking, "Is it nearly over yet?"

It is strange when you bow your head to pray
that you can't find the words you want to say.
But you can jabber on and on without an end
when you are spending time talking to a friend.

It is strange how difficult one chapter is to read
in the Bible each day as on His Word you feed.
You spend that time with a novel in your hand
agreeing with the author, this book is so grand.

When at the concert, you want the front row
but the back row at church whenever you go.
It is strange how we need to know of an event
so we can include it into how time will be spent.

We drink in what magazines and newspapers say
without any comparison to the Bible today.
We often repeat gossip, knowing it is not true.
Do any of these things seem strange to you?

Jesus Is Our Source

There are stories of Jesus feeding five thousand men
and sometimes included the women and children, too.
We find that mentioned in all four of the gospels.
It was put there for us to learn what we should do.

This massive assembly was facilitated that day
by the orderly arrangement of those that would dine.
And the disciplined delivery of the dedicated disciples
who hastened to feed them so all would be fine.

This makes us now wonder how it all happened.
Where did the supply of food keep repeating?
How did the disciples keep bringing it to them
and have leftovers from their plenty of eating?

Were the serving platters supernaturally engineered
like the widow's barrel of wheat many years ago?
And the cruse of oil that replenished itself
so as not to run out, being full to the overflow.

However, I have now come to the conclusion,
I think that when the basket was empty of bread
or the platter of fish was empty as could be,
they ran back to Jesus who filled it again instead.

Supply ran low, they went to the source for more.
They would hasten back to feed those in the field.
Even today .we must do the very same thing.
Jesus is also our source if to Him we will but yield.

Jesus Loves Us This Much

A little child begins their prayer
with hands outstretched they say,
"Jesus, I love You this much,
You guide me on my way."

"You give me what is needed
as I live my life for You.
I want You to know, there is
nothing for You I would not do."

This prayer is prayed today,
then the hands are folded in,
fingers clasped, head is bowed,
a silent prayer will now begin.

In the vision of the children,
they sit upon the Savior's knee,
knowing He reads every thought,
enjoying their every humble plea.

A special smile comes upon His face.
He nods His head, agreeing with them.
The words need not even be said.
He loves that they come to Him.

As we outstretch our arms to Him
to say, "Jesus, this much I love You."
He too stretched His arms open wide
in crucifixion, proving He loves us, too.

Elvis "Raz" Stephens

Jump Right In

The trash collectors come once a week.
That is good because trash does reek.
They take it away no more to be seen.
That helps you keep your place all clean.

The time is set as to when they come.
So, fill the can with that last little crumb.
And they will empty it as is planned.
You will be rid of all that is canned.

Mark your calendar so you'll not forget.
If you miss your day, you will be upset.
By next week it will be full for sure.
That awful stink will be hard to endure.

The housewife knew it was the day.
But she was piddling her time away.
She heard them coming down the street.
She tried to hurry, their schedule to meet.

Her housecoat flapping, she comes on the run.
Her hair in curlers and her makeup undone.
She says, "Am I too late for the trash again?"
"No Ma'am, go ahead and jump right in!"

Just Don't Like It

I see lots of posts on Facebook
where people ask for you to like.
But you kindly shake your head.
That one button you cannot strike.

You may be indifferent somewhat
with what it says or it shows.
You're not in complete agreement
and you do not care who knows.

Some things you immediately like.
On others the ice is really thin.
You are not compelled to respond.
Just do not hit the 'Like' then.

I oft find myself just reading
and looking at each and every post.
But I don't click the 'Like' button
unless I like it the very most.

You can post some pretty pictures.
I will agree that I like them most.
Just because I don't hit 'Like'
doesn't mean you should not post.

When I see that someone has written,
"Would you like my post, oh please?"
It is not that I just don't like it,
I just don't respond to any of these!

Elvis "Raz" Stephens

Just Let Them Be

There are many fruits on the experience tree.
Some have come at great expense
while others hanging there were free.

Some have a tasty odor and smell sweet.
Others are quite pungent.
Those are ones we wish not to repeat.

People also hang there in clear view.
We want them to be gone.
'Twas a bad experience they brought to you.

The experience tree just keeps on growing.
Getting bigger all the while.
Enlarged by mistakes we are sowing.

Vengeance would be our first reaction.
Seeing what is hanging there.
But it's not ours to seek satisfaction.

Fruit is the result of what has been sewn.
We bring it upon ourselves.
When we see it, we wish we'd only known.

The fruit is now witness against you and me.
Viewed as stinking, sour, or sweet.
We are judged by what the people see.

We cannot pick the bad fruit off the tree.
Pull it down and cast it away.
Experiences are better if we just let them be.

Kinfolk and Country Livin'

When back on the farm, our time was spent,
we didn't realize what things really meant
nor how wonderful was our time there.
We had something special but didn't care.

It seems we only wanted to hasten the day,
when we would be old enough to get away,
we dreamed back then of a far-off place.
The farm no longer would see our face.

This working from sunup until the sunset
would be left behind as far as we could get.
It was okay for our mom and dad to do
but it wasn't something we wanted to pursue.

When high school was finished, off we took
to bigger and better places to have a look.
We found things different than we supposed.
Those bigger places were more enclosed.

When vacation time came, we'd be so glad
hurrying back to see our mom and dad
to enjoy the life we once were given
to our kinfolk and that good country livin'.

Learning

"Take my yoke upon you and learn of me…" (Matt 11:29a)

Most were sixteen when we learned to drive.
Ever since we got that license, it became a factor.
Some may have been even just a little bit older
unless we grew up on a farm, then it was a tractor.

But my mind goes to a different kind of driving.
The different levels that I had to learn
to be successful in the sharing of the gospel,
to drive it home to the listener who did yearn.

I learned there are different levels of drivers:
those who do not know where to steer,
the ones who know they are not now able
and have made a wreck of all that's near,

then the ones who has taken driver's ed
and are now aware of those around that are lost.
Yet their mind is thinking of many dozen things.
It's dangerous to ride with them for it just may cost.

Learning the way of Christ is a lifetime thing.
You're to learn and practice what you've been taught
so that others can be advantaged by your driving.
Learning that they too are now being sought.

"Take My yoke upon you and learn of Me."
His truths are to be studied, as we discern
we can all be useful in His salvation offered,
as we take His yoke upon us and we learn.

Lessons Learned In Life

Never regret a day in your life.
The good days, happiness will give.
Bad days will give you experience.
Worst days give you lessons to live.

The best days give you memories
that you will never ever forget.
Each day that you live will be,
hopefully, one you will not regret.

Smile at the day God has given.
Take note there's only so many.
Do not fret little misfortunes
and today there will not be any.

You step out and step forward
and go on your merry way
knowing and being assured that
life lessons to be learned today.

You never get too old to learn.
If you slow down and observe,
there are many life lessons for us
that will assist us as we serve.

Try to learn something every day.
Life will teach us a new lesson.
Our best ability is availability as
we learn to be a special blessin'.

Let His Love Work

Though sometimes great be the cost,
the good we do is never lost.
Each kindly act we do is but a seed we sew.
As the seed will take its root,
in time it will bear its fruit,
and will attend us on our path below.

Take your cares to Jesus now.
With the when, and where, and how.
Let your trust in Him be all complete.
Let His love work within your soul
as you take the servant role
spending time in worship at His feet.

The works we do in Jesus' name
will cause us not to be the same.
As we receive each blessing from above,
consider what the Lord has done.
And thank Him for each faithful one.
Ask Him to teach us how to love.

Let's Go Exploring

Have you ever had the opportunity
to go exploring into the woods unbidden,
venturing down by the creek and bluffs
with caves that seem to be hidden.

It might have been a little scary.
But you wanted to go there any way.
Either alone or with someone else,
you entreated it by calling it 'play'.

The laurel leaves were a deep green
and their flowers had a wonderful smell.
You made sure you drank that in
so you could make sure to tell.

The indents back under the cliffs
where the earth had hallowed out,
you thought they were made by Indians.
You did not have nary a doubt.

You looked for a muscadine vine
hoping they would be ripe right now.
You might have to climb for them
but you would pick them anyhow.

What a great way to spend a day,
Seeing and doing what you'd never done,
You knew you'd enjoy this adventure,
Exploring the woods was so much fun,

Elvis "Raz" Stephens

Life Is Difficult, Regardless

When you ask someone how they're doing,
they may take the time to tell you stuff.
But mostly they will only say that they
are doing okay or at least well enough.

Do people really want to hear it all,
about what is happening in your life?
Do they want to take the time to listen
about your struggles and your strife?

If you tell them, it has been difficult
to go a mile making it inch by inch.
Regardless of whatever you tell them,
they just may think it was a cinch.

You and I both know the truth no less,
at times we find it even hard to go.
We feel okay or we think we do
but difficulties come, as we all know.

Life is difficult, regardless of our best.
We must give our all just to get through.
It is what we individually achieve
regardless of what anyone can do.

So, let's stay positive in our thinking
and go about doing all things good.
We know life is difficult, regardless,
even when we do the things we should.

Long Time No See

You see a friend coming toward you
and you give them a huge smile.
You may say, "Long time no see.
"I haven't seen you in a while."

It's good to have a friendship
and to have it be renewed.
I would much rather be seen
than to just be viewed.

Being a friend and having a friend
are not necessarily the same.
I don't think you can have one
just because they know your name.

An acquaintance says you know them
as to who you think they are.
That doesn't mean they're friendly.
They could be different by far.

A friend is someone who has
your best interest at heart.
They will always encourage you,
build you up from the start.

To have friend, you have to be a friend.
It's not that difficult to do.
I will count you as one of mine.
And I will be a friend to you.

Elvis "Raz" Stephens

Lost In The Woods

Have you ever been lost in the woods?
Maybe you just went for a little stroll
and soon you were turned around
with no way out, bless your poor soul.

You whistled and screamed very loud
but there came back not even an echo.
You stood there momentarily puzzled
trying to decide which way to go.

You thought you'd been this way before.
It did seem familiar to you at the start.
But now you are hopelessly lost
and now you're becoming faint of heart.

Maybe you should've paid more attention
when you were young and in the Scouts.
Which side of the tree did moss grow?
In a while, maybe I'll figure this out.

Then all at once you see an opossum.
You begin to follow it before it is gone.
And pretty soon as if by magic,
you're in the middle of the road alone.

Make-up Applied

Are make-up and camouflage basically the same,
even though it is called by a different name?
Each can be used to cover up what is being hid.
But not really hiding anything that you did.

Make-up may be helpful, when properly applied.
It may even be used when you need to hide.
Something you think others may not need to see
so, you camouflage it with make-up easy as can be.

Everyone that we see wears one or the other.
Not that they're trying to fool one another.
But it has become custom and the thing to do.
Not that it really matters to me or to you.

Even as ugly as I am I don't see the need
to cover up with make-up, it tends to impede.
Those products are costly and I couldn't afford.
So, I just go with what I was given by the Lord.

Wearing camouflage is just to be different it seems.
People can still see you in spite of your dreams.
What I am trying to say is that I do not care
if you do or you don't in whatever you wear.

March Madness

Well, here we are. It's that time of year again
when all the selected teams are trying to win.
They will be on many channels of your set.
Any one of the games you will be able to get.

It wasn't long ago when we had but a few.
You had to choose which was best for you.
But now you can surf to your heart's desire
and find each game that you do require.

There's no real underdog for which to root.
Some of the games you will not give a hoot.
But as you daily watch a favorite will arise.
You'll stick with them, they may win the prize.

Each conference has its own team vying.
Giving it their best and always be trying.
You cannot go by the wins or the losses.
Each team seems to have their player bosses.

Referees are ready, crowds are anticipating.
It all starts tonight, there is no more waiting.
The ball will be tossed and the tip is made.
For the next three weeks, games will be played.

March Madness is on and it will be exciting.
The games are happening and so inviting.
So let us be prepared and rested and willing.
Man oh man, this will be overly thrilling.

Memories Make You Happy

Someone quoted this fact on Facebook today,
"While looking at pictures from back in the day
as they dug through their pictures stored there
in that old album preserved with much care."

There were pictures of themselves then as a youth
having fun, being silly, and acting very uncouth.
And, of course, the birthdays they celebrated,
seeing again family members who are related.

The pictures show the growth year after year
all the way up to where they are right here.
Each brings a big smile and makes us very glad.
Oh, what great fun we now remember we had.

I am sure at times, we all like to reminisce
as we think about the time that we did this.
Looking at the picture will bring it right back.
The memory it relives as it fills in our lack.

Then comes the marriages to whom and when.
We love to be reminded of those times again.
Those happy days and happy times we enjoyed.
Using them again today to fill up the void.

Memories make us happy as we can tell,
looking back on the good times as we dwell.
Overcoming sadness, only good things we see.
Reliving great memories, happy as can be.

Elvis "Raz" Stephens

Mommy's Work Was Never Done

My mommy was a hardworking woman.
She was always busy, constantly on the go.
Working in the house, or out in the field,
doing all she could to help us kids to grow.

Up in the morning for breakfast so early
making sure that each of us were well fed
because we would need our energy
for the long workday that lay ahead.

She'd work with us in the field in the morning,
then go back to the house just before noon.
That would make all of us kids happy because
we knew dinner would be ready very soon.

Tuesday was her planned wash day.
That old ringer washer went all day.
She'd slice and dice that old soap bar
making soapy water to wash the dirt away.

Drawing water to make sure there was plenty
to wash clothes and then also to rinse.
Making sure all of her kids were kept clean.
I have not seen a harder worker ever since.

The example set before us by mommy
still lives on in each of us to attest.
Though Mommy's work here was never done,
it's now over and she has gone to her rest.

Mother's Logic

My mother taught me about the WEATHER, so clear,
"Child, it looks like a tornado has hit in here."
She taught me about RELIGION, no doubt,
"Look at that carpet, you best pray that'll come out!"

Mother taught me 'bout TIME TRAVEL, so to speak,
"I'll knock you into the middle of next week."
My mother taught me about OSMOSIS somehow,
"Eat your supper, shut your mouth right now."

She taught me about the 'CIRCLE of LIFE' tis true,
"I brought you into the world, I can take you out too."
She taught me all about ENVY, by what she said,
"All children want mothers like you have instead."

Mother taught me about RECEIVING, you bet,
"When we get home, you know what you will get."
Mother taught me about GENEALOGY, ever so mild,
"Shut that door. Were you born in a barn, my child?"

She taught me about JUSTICE, more times than a few,
"One day you'll have kids who'll be just like you."
My mother taught me about STAMINA, on and on,
"You will sit there until your spinach is gone."

My mother taught me about IRONY, no doubt,
"Keep crying! I'll give you something to cry about!"
Mother taught me about LOGIC, I cannot deny,
She ended with, "Because I said so, that's why."

Elvis "Raz" Stephens

My Life Is All Surround Sound

At times, I seem to hear a voice
that says, "Go ahead and do it."
Then at times it will say to me,
"That was wrong and you knew it."

Sometimes it speaks ever so slight.
Other times it is loud and strong.
If I will but pause for the cause,
it doesn't say do what is wrong.

My mind goes in many directions.
Mostly each is a good thought.
Seldom do I think on things
that I know I should not.

A little tune will make me smile.
I do enjoy hearing them played.
The words seem to say my mind.
It's the same I want relayed.

I step out into this ole world
and I take life as it comes to me.
I change what I can if I can
to have a pleasing melody.

To get along with all others,
keeping things simple as can be,
I try to face the music but
it is all surround sound to me.

My Obit

I teasingly say, "I'll check the obit,
and see if my name is listed in it."
But that is said just trying to amuse,
I am in no hurry the obit to use.

But there'll be new ones listed today
who have recently passed away.
We read the notice, shaking our head.
Someone we knew is listed as dead.

Hopefully, we can be glad and rejoice.
One day again we will hear their voice.
There is no reason for us to be sad
as we remember the good times we had.

Their testimony will cause us to smile.
We'll see them again after a short while.
They said they'd look for us up there.
If we but only believe and we prepare.

My obit will tell you that I am gone.
It'll share with you the life I have known.
If you trust what it says that I am okay,
then you will see me again one fine day.

So go forth and conquer all that you will.
Hang on and hold on for that day until
there'll be good things written 'bout you
and you will live on in your life anew.

My Young Friend, Nicholas (Nov. 1994-Dec. 2021)

Here a few days after Christmas has taken place,
my young friend, Nicholas, gets to see Jesus face to face.
Nick would lighten your heart in a short while.
Hearing his quick laugh and seeing his big old smile.

He was a jovial big man with a great big heart.
All who met him loved him right from the start.
He was gentle and tender in all of his doing,
putting others first in whatever he was pursuing.

He loved his family and his church family, too,
eagerly partaking in all the things he could do.
It goes without saying he will surely be missed.
When counting friends, he's at the top of the list.

We saw Nicholas grow from birth to become a man.
He professed Christ as Savior and followed His plan.
We are all saddened with Nick's passing away.
But we are assured we'll see him again one day.

So, goodbye my friend Nicholas, but not for long.
Your testimony will help us to remain strong.
Your leaving has caused us to be full of emotion.
But we can now celebrate your heavenly promotion.

From Velva Jo and Raz:
We loved this young man very much and are so saddened
by his leaving us so young on Dec. 30, 2021

Never Say Never

As soon as you say they never would,
they will never, never, like never before.
We think they are above doing that
but soon they do it again even more.

The teacher asks, "Where is your child?"
My child has never missed any school.
Of course, I respond, "Aren't they there?
My child would never break the rule."

The game is designed to build confidence.
You may lose but you will also grow.
Everybody cannot be a big winner.
When you're young that's good to know.

But cheating often comes to the front.
People want so very badly to win it.
They never seem to get over the loss.
Although they were never really in it.

When we give our oath, we often say,
"I promise never to do or to say that."
But that 'never' comes to haunt so fast.
Soon that's exactly where we are at.

I am trying to stop saying, "I never would."
Never saying 'never' is my intended win.
So, I give you my solemn promise today
that I will never ever say never again.

Elvis "Raz" Stephens

No Fun Today

Today is not a day of fun
but a time to get things done.
Long enough I let things go.
Today they must come undertow.

Things are scattered, floor's a mess,
time to vacuum, I confess,
it doesn't take all that long
to put things back where they belong.

Straighten and tidy up a bit.
Housework gives me a bonified fit.
But I will do it mostly because
it's breaking all cleanliness laws.

So clean and polish, spray and wipe,
though I don't get why all the hype.
So, what if my house is a big mess.
I can live with that, nonetheless.

But if I do what some others do,
it'll soon be looking most brand new.
Today I'll spend what time as I can
making this house look all spic-n-span.

It is not fun trying to be this neat.
Thank goodness I don't oft repeat.
But today I want to get-er-done.
Knowing that today will not be fun.

No Problem

Today, instead of saying "Thank you,"
people say "No problem" in response.
That just seems to me that we are
not as thoughtful as we were once.

We hold the door open for ladies.
They hurry past us without a grin.
We want them to know we care.
Their big concern is to just get in.

If we give someone a compliment,
they just go on their merry way.
Our "THANK YOU" to get attention.
"No problem" is oft what they say.

Have we become so inconsiderate
that a simple kindness is too tough?
Ought we not show our gratitude?
Is a "No problem" good enough?

If to all this you have no problem,
then that is likewise okay with me.
I'll still use "Please" and "Thank you."
"No problem" you'll not hear or see.

Not All Wounds Are Visible

Each of us has a memory we hold
of something that easily comes to mind.
We try to forget all the bad things,
but peace is most difficult to find.

Sometimes it is a wound to our ego
when we get put in our place.
Though insignificant to others,
those times are then hard to face.

A wound takes time to heal up.
Some stay open for quite a while.
The scab is so easily torn off.
We have to go that extra mile.

Even though we pride our toughness
and think we are beyond all that.
Things come back to haunt us
bringing us down where we are at.

Outside hurts can be forgiven
and the wound hopefully will heal
as we try to look past the doing,
but yet the wound is so real.

Some do not care that they wounded.
They say, "I've done no harm to you."
We must practice internal healing.
Not all wounds are visible, tis true.

Ode To A Cat

Oh, to be a cat.
To lay around all day getting fat.
Oooops, too late, I've already done that.

To follow its feeder
like playing follow the leader
reminding you that you just may need her.

They will not play fetch.
They will lay in the sun and stretch.
Anything moving they will try to catch.

They will not let you sleep
making sure early hours you keep.
They want their food bowl filled to the heap.

It's almost as if they can talk.
They get under your feet as you walk.
And whatever you tell them to do, they will balk.

What a life of leisure they enjoy.
They will give lots of love for a new toy.
Then they will look for something to destroy.

Oh, to have the life of a cat,
living carefree so people are jealous at.
Just maybe so, but I'm not too sure about that.

Old People

You can spot old men as far as you can see 'em.
One day we may be fortunate enough to be 'em.
They stand tall when the anthem is being played.
Their hand and hat is over their heart then laid.

They remember the wars that we've been through.
The atomic age, jet age, and the moon landing, too.
If you bump into an old person while out and about,
they will be the first to then apologize, no doubt.

If you should pass an old man on the street,
they will tip their hat to the ladies they meet.
They'll go out of their way to open the door for you.
Old men automatically know what's best to do.

They will walk near the curb, protection to provide,
allowing the women to always walk on the inside.
Old men get embarrassed when cursing is heard.
They hate when someone takes in vain God's word.

They do not like the filth that is on the movie screen.
For the sake of the children, this should never be seen.
They never brag unless it's about one of their own
children or grandchildren that are now grown.

Old men remove their hats when they sit to eat
in respect of the guests and the ladies they meet.
This country needs our old men, as we all know,
for their pride in their country and values they show.

One Thing Is Needful

"One thing is needful:
Mary has chosen that good part,
Which shall not be taken away from her."
She loves and worships with her heart. Luke 10:42

Jesus is telling Martha that there is one thing
more important than all others we can know.
It is the choicest morsel and the most essential.
And Mary has chosen that and will now show.

Martha represents those who are encumbered
with much serving and doing what is good.
But while she's doing that, she is neglecting
the best thing and not worshipping as she could.

We, like her, have often gotten all caught up
in doing the work, thus the Lord we've neglected.
Not remembering that in all work we do,
the Lord of the work is to be reflected.

We need to take the time to sit at His feet.
Mary did this and was blessed the more.
Listening to what He had to say to all.
She wanted to do His will like ne'er before.

Worship must be sensible and balanced, too.
Our hearts stirred and an enlightened mind.
Worship is sincere, pleasing, and acceptable.
Then it will be Spirit-filled as we all will find.

Other People's Opinion

Aren't you glad that other people's opinion
does not matter nor change who you are?
You are now saved and in Christ Jesus
though you still may carry a visible scar.

Jealousy and envy are such ugly things.
Those emotions are so easily found.
Those haters are always going to hate.
Still the imitators want you around.

Gossips are gonna gossip and also squawk.
It doesn't take any doing to get them going.
People are going to talk no matter what.
It doesn't matter to them if they are knowing.

But Jesus knows our heart and how we feel.
He knows all those people who seek to abuse.
But He will turn it all around for our good.
He tells us to pray for those who spitefully use.

Pencil or Eraser

I trust this is a good suggestion
that I now share with each of you.
It is meant to be taken positively.
Something that we each can do.

We can each of us be a pencil
and write about something good
and add it into our own life.
If we'd take the time and would.

It could be a few do's and don'ts.
Doing addition but not subtraction.
Noting the things that come to mind
that will need our further action.

A pencil can be used to compliment
and to say "thank you" for a gift.
There are many things you can write
to give someone a special lift.

Maybe you think you're not a pencil.
You do not care about any of these.
If you can't write into life a positive,
then try not to be an eraser, PLEASE.

Elvis "Raz" Stephens

Perception Is The Key

Some could be given an entire field
of roses and only see it is well thorned.
Others could be given a single weed
and only see a wildflower adorned.

Perception is the key component
to gratitude that we each see.
And gratitude is the key component
for the joy that comes to you and me.

They say that if you wish to be happy,
then happiness you must receive.
It all ties in to having perception..
You have to be able to perceive

I believe today is going to be great.
The sun will shine even if clouds I see.
I believe the temperature will be mild.
Because perception is the key.

Goldilocks said it in her story,
"Not too hot and not too cold."
And we have all repeated that
when the forecast of the day is told.

Perception is but what we make it.
It can be bad, but we wish for good.
Take it in and be glad you have it.
Perception is the key, if you would.

Plain Enough

Open your Bible and be immediately presented
with the workings of God that have not relented.
He made the earth and the heavens in six days.
And He therein acquaints us in all of His ways.

He has been at that job of sustaining His creation.
He fashioned us so that we could have relation.
He created us all in His own image, in part,
that means we also can create in our heart.

For what are our legs, hands, and minds used,
He wants all of those things to not be abused.
He expects those tools to be actively enrolled
bringing Him glory by doing what we are told.

God put man in the garden to work every day.
To dress it and keep it in His own special way.
The garden needed working, man needed work.
Our Creator worked, therefore, we shouldn't shirk.

Work is not a punishment for sin, as we've heard.
It is not because of the fall, we learn in His word.
Paradise needed the hands of man to be involved.
God ordained that and His purpose was solved.

When sin entered the earth, it hindered all things.
Man would now work hard for the reward it brings.
We can be slothful and try to not do His will.
But the way of the righteous is made plain still.

Elvis "Raz" Stephens

Plowing The Field

As I was plowing out the field,
many big ole worms it did reveal.
I'd hurriedly gather up each one.
Was going fishing when I was done.

The old mule would just plod along
pulling the plow. She was so strong.
No hurry just a good steady pace.
She was not in any kind of race.

When I'd bend over, a worm to gather,
she'd hold tight upon the leather.
I'd grab the worm, put it in my jaw.
the craziest thing you ever saw.

A neighbor stopped, asked me, "why
was I gathering worms," as he passed by.
I spit them out into my hand
so I could help him understand.

I told him I wanted to fish in the brook.
I needed worms so I could bait my hook.
So, in my mouth I was saving them.
That must have seemed most odd to him.

"Why not put them into your pocket then?"
I spit the worms into my hand again,
"Cause, I want to handle them with care
AND I carry my chew tobaccer in there."

Portrayed On TV

Perhaps you are like me these days
and watch entirely too much TV.
There is a show to catch my eye
and it briefly will appeal to me.

If I decide that I don't like that one,
I switch to something more appealing.
Maybe this one I can stick with
if its stars and plots aren't too revealing.

These shows make me pause and think
and wonder if life is at all this way.
Gone are the days when life was simple.
Now all is made for a television play.

Westerns are turned into a series.
You have to come back every week
to see what else has happened.
They keep your interest at the peak.

People seem to enjoy other's problems.
There's too much misery for me.
I'd rather be happy and not always sad.
Not doom and gloom portrayed on TV.

We each have our most special night.
The shows are what we want to see.
I'm not a doctor but I can prescribe
one that is portrayed on my TV.

Reciprocity

There are things we can exchange for mutual benefit
to other people whom we know who are in need of it.
We trust that we will get like value in return.
But sometimes we receive a hard lesson to learn.

Advantage can be taken as easy as can be
when we do not get full reciprocity.
We look for something similar to obtain
but there's no resemblance in whate'er we gain.

In the relationship, we both come to agree
what I give to you and you then give to me.
We allow each other to have the same right
and trust return of same without any slight.

Friendships have been broken over this no less.
They promise reciprocity but it turns into a mess.
Arguing doesn't seem to resolve a hand-shake deal.
Neither one will give an inch, neither will repeal.

To 'reciprocate' means action to even up the score
of what either has been doing, things going on before.
But 'reciprocity' has way much more feeling in it.
If we will but keep our word, both sides can win it.

Resting In The Dust

In the book of Genesis, it is found,
God made man from dust of the ground.
And breathed into him life's very breath
which would sustain him until his death.

"It is appointed unto man once to die."
We just don't know the when nor why.
But the time will come in which we must
each be surrendered back into the dust.

Let there be no sorrow for the decision made.
For of this death, we're not to be afraid.
When this earthly body is now interred,
not the soul and spirit according to His Word.

Those two shall live forever and then,
one day in Heaven we'll see them again.
In the image of God was man created
having peace in death can't be overstated.

If we learn to trust Him with all our heart,
there'll be joy when from earth we depart.
As our loved one rests here in repose,
they'll rise again because Christ arose.

Now shall the dust return unto dust again
and the spirit returns to God. AMEN
Let us who are alive give unto Him praise
and live for Him the rest of our days.

Saturday Coffee In My PJs

I do not consider it a waste of time.
If it's Saturday and you find that I'm
still just sitting with coffee in hand,
wearing my PJs, and feeling grand.

Usually, my Saturday is an off day
when I can just sit passing time away.
And drink my coffee, cup after cup,
being glad that I could even be up.

No hurry, no worry, just relaxing.
Doing nothing that could be taxing.
Checking out the TV guide to see
which ball games appeal to me.

Wearing PJs all day, I have found
is great when snow's on the ground.
Having no need to really go outside.
I love the taste coffee does provide.

So, I just sit here and smile as I sip.
Wearing PJs makes me look hip.
I almost choked at that last line.
But recovered fast and now I'm fine.

This being retired sure has its merit.
Saturday coffee in PJs, I'm all fer-it.
I am not lazy, or at least I hope.,
Saturday coffee in PJs helps me cope.

Self-Hate Will Radiate

When you think so little of yourself
that others can see it right away,
you do not care what they think
nor do you care 'bout what they say.

You will do as you want to do
whether it's thought good or bad.
If other folks try to get involved,
it seems to only make you mad.

You think you know what is best.
You do not care how bad it looks.
If you suffer, then let it be so
whether good or bad in their books.

They may in time think as you do.
They may take on your attitude
and soon will be unloving souls,
begin to say things that are rude.

We affect those that interact
and cause them to do contrary.
If they end up as we have done,
why is it that we should worry.

We say we are not their keepers.
We do not answer for their fate.
If we only stop to realize, that
soon our self-hate will radiate.

Sense and Sensibility

A faculty by which the body perceives
is said to be a sense
or a feeling that something is the case
and so we react hence.

Sensibility is thus described as
the way things are believed.
We could make a case that both
are today being deceived.

I trust that it's not only me
that tends to think this way.
Our sense and sensibility
have disappeared today.

Maybe it's just a play on words
but I think that it is true.
We are not using either one
the way we used to do.

We've become somewhat immune
to what is now occurring.
Just letting be what is to be,
we are no longer worrying.

But I am growing more concerned.
I just wish that we could see
how fast we are now losing
our sense and sensibility.

Shopping Cart Woes

Yesterday I went shopping over to the mart.
Bought many items and used a shopping cart.
As I studied other people, I was very amused
about their carelessness with the cart they used.

They wouldn't pay attention nor give a tiny smile
as they cut you off in the middle of the aisle.
Other shoppers seemed to own the right-of-way,
a miserable look about them, and not a word to say.

They'd stop their cart in front of you to impede.
Reaching over you for something they would need.
No "excuse me for a moment, if you please."
Not even "I just need to grab up one of these."

Shopping carts can be dangerous, as we truly know
especially in the hands of those on the go,
as if they're in a hurry to get to the checkout line
where they will have to wait long enough to dine.

When you get outside to unload, there you will find
carts scattered everywhere by shoppers left behind.
One guy put his items into his car and then
he reloaded the cart with his trash from within.

Carts should be taken to their designated spot.
But people do not seem to care about that a lot.
Having been taught better, I know where the cart goes.
Woe unto shoppers and their shopping cart woes?

Simply Put

A simple good morning goes a long way.
Or I love you, have a great day.
So I am sending all three to you
as you travel along on your way.

I don't write to offend with my words
but to simply get my words out there
where you can read them and think
and then decide if you even care.

When all our words have been censured
and all our freedoms are then gone,
only then will we fully discover
why we're feeling so all alone.

If it's important to you, you'll find a way.
If not, you will find an excuse.
We learned a lot through past experiences
when good manners were still in use.

We spend too much time trying to fit in,
knowing we were born to stand out.
And way too much time listening to people
who know not what they are talking about.

Most of these thoughts come from Facebook.
And we can see our society's in a rut.
The negative has displaced the positive.
That is what we all see today, Simply Put.

Sitting At The Table With Your Judas

Inspired by Bro. Harold Nobles' message on Nov 28, 2021.

Do you feel good about being angry once more?
Do you feel the need to slam another door?
Bitterness seems to hang on and will not budge.
You're not yet ready to forgive them of this grudge.

They did something to you out of vengeful spite.
You have no intention of allowing them make it right.
And you are not going to offer them your hand.
That would be a kindly gesture far too grand.

But we see in the story of Jesus' very last meal
how toward His betrayer, Judas, He did feel.
He told His disciples He'd be betrayed and die.
Judas "<u>Feigned Sorrow</u>" in asking, "Master, is it I?"

Once the plan was put in motion, Judas didn't stop.
Jesus said it will be he who does the "<u>Figurative Sop</u>."
His bitterness well hidden in worthiness of his name,
he took the price they offered in his "<u>Forgotten Shame</u>."

In the garden, Jesus was speaking, the guard came to seek
and His betrayer saying "Master", kissed Him on the cheek.
Jesus knew that it must be this way in the end.
In "<u>Fervent Salutation</u>" Jesus calls His betrayer "Friend."

When we have a betrayer that careth not to destroy,
do we use forgiveness and kindness to employ?
If that is our deep desire, we ask Jesus to enable
when our Judas sits with us at our very own table.

Skills That I Possess

If I mentioned that I have real skills,
you would think I am trying to brag.
You may also have a few of these
odd skills contained within my bag.

There is one little skill I have
that other people seem to share.
It surprises me when it happens.
I can actually choke on air.

This skill that I now mention
is one I that can't ignore.
I have a tendency to trip
over nothing in or on the floor.

When it comes to the stairs,
my skill is most renown.
I am extra careful because
I can fall up instead of down.

It is not my intent to brag.
I have mastered all of these.
This is but a few of the ones
that come naturally with ease.

Elvis "Raz" Stephens

Smarter Than He Looked

There is a sweet story of a young boy
who appeared by all to be very shy.
He would just stand and listen to others
and never would ask the reason why.

He went to the store one day with Mom.
He mostly watched as she walked about.
The store proprietor watched him closely
trying to figure the young man out.

He did not do what other boys do:
pick things up and hold them a while.
All he did was just meander around.
Never really giving even a smile.

After fulfilling the mother's order,
the man invited the boy to some candy
that was right there in a visible jar.
To reach in it would be quite handy.

But the boy hesitated and did not.
He just stood there staring at the floor.
So, the owner sought to offer him,
"Take a handful," he did implore.

Seeing that the boy would not take any,
he reached in and pulled out a lot.
The mother later asked him why he didn't.
He said, "He's got bigger hands than I got."

Some Are Still Searching

"And some believed the things that were spoken,
and some believed not." Though it was plain.
You will always find that to be the truth.
That in their lost condition, some people remain.

Some are still searching, knowing not for what.
Searching for purpose or peace they have not.
"Those that seek Me early shall find Me."
Are His words of reality for what we then got.

Some are still silent, and they walk away
from God's man, His message, His salvation plan.
Not hearing the man nor his message for them,
they continue on, thinking it's the best they can.

"The LORD is far from the wicked," Proverbs says,
"but He will yet hear the righteous prayer."
If man goes down in silence, there'll be no praise.
His separation will continue each day and each hour.

We're reminded it matters not what car we drive
or the size of the house in which we reside.
It matters not if all our clothes are in style.
Have we accepted salvation that God did provide?

You can continue searching if that is your wish,
or stop and partake of His goodness and grace.
Do not reject the Savior and refuse His salvation.
Your searching will stop if you will seek His face.

Elvis "Raz" Stephens

Some Days

Some days life is very hard.
Some days it is just too tough.
Some days you want it all.
Some you just can't get enough.

Some days go by too fast.
Some days are so very slow.
Some days are confusing
and you don't know where to go.

Some days you have the best plan.
Some days your plans go awry.
You expected all to be okay.
Some days you're left to wonder why.

Some days it is easy to wear a smile.
Some days all you can do is frown.
Remember what your Momma told you,
"Turn that frown upside down."

Some days you seem a bit too moody.
Some days your mood is light.
Some days it all comes together.
Some days everything goes right.

Some day when this life is over,
we've departed and gone away.
Someday we'll live eternally
with our dear Savior— Some Day.

Some Little Ole Something

When it seems that you are stuck
and just can't seem to move on,
your memory may be frozen
and things won't leave you alone.

Or your mind just may be blank.
Nothing will come into view.
Because some little ole something
is blocking and bothering you.

Maybe it is some little ole something
that some uncaring person has said
that got stuck there in your mind
and is still sitting there in your head.

People say things without meaning,
without any thought nor intention.
They callously blurt it right out,
that little ole something they mention.

But maybe we can turn things around
by taking their minds another way,
giving them much encouragement
by some little ole something we say.

Little ole somethings will add up quick
when we use them as we ought should.
Be positive in all we share with others.
Make it some little ole something good.

Elvis "Raz" Stephens

Some Scars Last a Lifetime

Some scars last a lifetime
but now this I promise you,
they will not keep you from
what you want and need to do.

You must be at peace with
the scars that are on hand
knowing there are many things
that we do not understand.

Why bad things seem to happen
to good people that we know.
Why we come down with illness.
Why are things always so.

Why someone betrayed us
as we walked side by side.
But we're not to get bitter
about the scars they provide.

Scars aren't here to hold you back.
They're reminders of Gods' grace.
Of what He brought you through
to this now much better place.

Some scars are very evident
lasting a lifetime in easy view.
Other scars are hidden away.
They're known only just to you.

Storms Are Temporary

Storms are only temporary.
Soon they will be passed.
They do however come.
Although they do not last.

We receive them for certain
not because of what is done.
But because they are part of
the race each of us must run.

Storms can be overpowering.
They bow us to the knee.
We all can rest assured that
they'll come to you and me.

Should they be allowed to win
and cause us to be afraid
or do we stand up more tall
not becoming overly dismayed.

If we know they are temporary,
then why do we cower in fear?
We can seek from God the answer,
He is always listening, ever near.

He will comfort us in our worry
when things are going wild
because storms are temporary.
He says, "I am here My child."

Elvis "Raz" Stephens

Stress and Duress, What a Mess No Less

You gave it all you had no less
and it yet turned out a big ole mess.
Now that causes you a lot of stress.
You're feeling somewhat in duress.

Is it that you ask yourself to do too much?
Somewhere you seem to lose your touch.
You over-stretch and over-extend,
then you're not pleased with the end.

Things were not so very well planned
with not enough resources at hand.
You just made an educated guess.
Now you are feeling much duress.

Stress seems to be a catchword today
when outside forces come into play.
You put much energy into it no less.
Things still end up in a great big mess.

Let me try encouraging you just a bit.
Don't let stress and duress come in and sit.
Keep striding on and let God bless.
You will overcome the mess no less.

Stubborn As A Mule

Different people have different motives
for each and all the things they do.
If you but stop and think a moment,
you'd say you are the same way, too.

Someone may try to convince you
to think or do things differently.
But you are set, you know what's best,
and you'll do it just the way you see.

Back on the farm, we had two mules.
They were different as night and day.
When you would try to get them 'gee',
they would decide 'haw' was the way.

Myrt and Maude were quiet a pair.
At times, neither would obey command..
They were stubborn as they could be.
They did not care to understand.

It is very hard to get anything done
when we don't pull at the same time.
It will be half-done or unfinished
when it could have been sublime.

It is a lot like that in God's work.
He has a plan and gives us a rule.
But we accomplish little or not at all
when we are as stubborn as a mule.

Elvis "Raz" Stephens

Text, Text, Text, so What is Next?

Why is it okay to text instead of call?
Why do they even bother you at all?
If people do not have time to chat,
why do they send you this or that?

To make a call only takes a minute.
But they use a text with nothing in it.
I even got one, 'twas short as could be.
All that it contained was "Call me."

If it is news worth sharing at all,
then they had best give me a call.
I can with assurance tell you that I'm
not gonna waste my valuable time.

You may still try to reach me by text.
But I can tell you what happens next.
You will have to call me any way
to tell me what you want to say.
I'm at BR549.

That Privilege Is Denied

The years have slowly added on.
Now our youth has up and gone.
Hopefully we are the wiser now.
We know what to do and how.

We aren't the same as before.
Not all slim and trim anymore.
But the soul is still there inside.
We use strength it does provide.

We have our pride and grace, too,
even after all we've been through.
Like a classic car we have our worth
gained from experiences on earth.

Youth had its exuberance and zest.
Our experience now shows the best.
We have lost some that we held dear.
They did not make it to be here.

When the opportunity is lost, it's gone.
Yet we still have to carry on alone.
Being older we are mostly satisfied.
For some, the privilege has been denied.

For those who are alive and well,
we need to now go forth and tell
so the wisdom of age can be applied.
For some, that privilege is denied.

The Bible Does Not Say That

There are some very common misquotes
that the Bible does not say anywhere.
We use them so very often when we talk.
People are sure they are included there.

"God never gives you more than you
can handle." People often will misquote
as if in the Bible God had made sure
that this line had certainly been wrote.

"If you can't say something nice,
don't say anything at all," we hear.
But we cannot find that written
because it isn't in there, nowhere near.

"To thine oneself be true..." sounds like
something Shakespeare would have used.
"God helps those who help themselves."
That line will cause us to be confused.

"Gaining your angel wings" is popular.
But it is not by works we have done
that will allow us to enter heaven
but belief in and on His begotten Son.

"Money is the root of all evil," we hear.
But it's the love of money this evil brings.
"Cleanliness is next to godliness," we're told,
but the Bible does not say these things.

The Blessing Of Obed Edom

There is a story in the Old Testament
that we hear and love to share.
It is about the Ark of the Covenant
and about its very special care.

King David was bringing it back home
but he had no house to provide.
So, unto the house of Obed Edom
we find that it was turned aside.

They were undecided what to do.
They needed a place it could rest.
So Obed Edom offered immediately
to house it and by it be blessed.

For three months there it remained.
His house was blessed beyond measure.
Soon word got back to King David
and he came to retrieve the treasure.

When they needed a resolution,
Obed Edom said, "Please use my home."
This invitation today is our example
of the many blessings that will come.

We invite the Lord to come unto us.
He will come and blessings will instill.
We'll find His goodness overflowing
to the fullness and He will overfill.

Elvis "Raz" Stephens

The Long And The Short Of It

Sometimes I write things very long
to say what I think I need to say.
Other times my thoughts are short.
My tendency is to be that way.

The thought comes and I must write
or I will soon lose it post haste.
So, I try to jot it down quickly
not wanting it to go to waste.

At times, long sentences are best
to get out the thought that's meant.
Other times they're short and sweet
to include all of the full intent.

Be it long or short, it will include
things with which you can identify.
I give it to you with its own rhyme.
Or at least I give it my best try.

Poems are meant to be very wordy.
They say things that make us smile.
We find ourselves nodding with them
bringing us joy for a little while.

So, if the poem is long or short
just try to enjoy and you will find,
at least the author's truly trying
to bring you joy and peace of mind.

The Most Challenging Battle
(Praying for our children)

The most challenging battle that we each face
is in praying for our children day by day.
We pray in dedication, giving them to God
and trusting they will not turn from the way.

We pray for salvation of their needy soul
that they will give in and give to God their life.
The importance of this can't be overstated.
Their living for Him will save them much strife.

We pray they will have some godly friends
who will help with the influence they bring.
Helping them to submit to God's will.
Always doing what is right in everything.

We will not forget to pray for their health
and their well-being as they interact each day.
That they will show forth good godly character.
And follow Jesus' example in all of the way.

Praying for their future is also important
for all decisions and especially for their mate.
In all things, they would wait with patience
being not in any hurry to seal their fate.

Pray for guidance and spiritual protection
in all the things they do and what they decide.
Lord, let them successfully face all challenges
that God would always be first and glorified.

The Older I Get

As I get older, I so often stop and pause
about what is happening and also the cause.
Never in my lifetime had this come into play.
I never thought I would see it as I see it today.

Being old is okay, as long as I can keep going.
I learn new things that are worth my knowing.
But after I have learned them, I tend to forget.
That just naturally happens the older I get.

I view things differently than I used to do.
So many new things that now come into view.
Nothing surprises me, even though it should.
Not all that new stuff is truly for our good.

Maybe you would say I am set in my ways.
I think we need more of those people these days.
Folk who will not give in just to go along.
It is those who help all others stay strong.

Yes, I am opinionated and not easily fooled,
showing my resistance when I'm overruled.
But I try not so quickly to be brought to fret.
I show my patience wisely the older I get.

Many things happen that cause me frustration
in dealing with this younger generation.
I will continue my helping them, you bet.
They need me more now as the older I get.

The Price of Gasoline

I'm sure all of you by now
know the price of gasoline.
It is now the highest that
we users have ever seen.

To fill up costs a pretty penny.
That's how the older folks talk.
If it is close enough to here,
I guess I'll just have to walk.

I put the hose into the tank
and watch the price go up.
I squeeze upon the nozzle hard
making sure I get that last sup.

To be able to go as before
would be ever so nice.
But now I stay close to home,
I don't want to pay that price.

Even when I use my card,
those pennies add up quick.
I'm okay until I have to pay.
Then it makes me sick.

We have to have gas I do reckon.
I'm not real sure what is the cure.
But I know the price makes me ill.
I have car-owner virus, I am sure.

Elvis "Raz" Stephens

The Road of Grief

We work very hard to build relationships
then one day in an instant they're gone.
We would bring them back if we could,
but it's probably better that we just go on.

Grief can be extra hard to work through.
It seems that it will not ever go away.
We think we have it mastered and then,
Bamm! It pops right back up one day.

Our mind is made to drink things in
and hold on to things we store in there.
We memorize and trust not to forget
those things we give unto its care.

We train ourselves to hold on to good,
not let the bad go along for the ride.
Always believing the best of one lost
as we try to let all our grief subside.

We wish there was a magic button
we could push and walk away with relief.
The longest walk we'll ever take
is the one down the road of grief.

The Things That I Have Now

Have you ever wanted something
that you had not yet obtained?
Did you patiently wait and wonder
if one day it would be gained?

Did you form a plan to get it
or just hope it'd come your way?
In the very recess of your mind
you thought, "I'll have that one day."

Have you wanted something so badly
you thought you could almost taste it?
You thought, "Oh, if only I had that,
I know I surely would not waste it."

We have all had those opportunities
to gain the things on each our lists.
We pretty much have now attained
what we've wanted if it does exist.

We find that things do not satisfy
and we have garnered up a pile.
They brought us momentary gladness
but that was only for a little while.

Today, I am so much more satisfied
because less seems more somehow.
Nothing can erase nor can it replace
the things that I have now.

Elvis "Raz" Stephens

The Wisdom of Old Age

They say with age comes wisdom.
You will know things in your heart.
By now I should be close enough
for that wisdom now to start.

But yet I find myself wondering
about stuff I ought to know.
Being puzzled at my old age.
When is that wisdom gonna show?

I sit and think and I ponder,
"Has it gotten any easier yet?
I have now aged accordingly
Is this all the wisdom that I get?"

I've had many experiences of life.
Each one has taught me some.
It's getting harder to patiently wait.
When's wisdom supposed to come?

I've tried to store things up to use
to pull from when it's time to show
but even at my advanced age,
I'm just not smart enough to know.

The Wrath to Come

There is a subject that seems not to bother some.
We try to avoid talking about, "The wrath to come."
People with fair understanding say that it is clear,
The saved will miss this because they are no longer here.

"The righteous is taken away from that evil wrath to come."
People forsake this and allow their minds to yet be numb.
This will be a direct act of God that takes place that day.
Only those who have believed will avoid going this way.

I am not a prognosticator, nor do I claim to be.
But if you read your Bible, it is very plain to see.
There are many tell-tale signs to show us very clear.
His coming is so imminent and is drawing ever near.

James says, "The judge stands ready at the door."
Our days are numbered and there'll not be many more.
Many times, many places, God's judgment has been poured
upon those who would not listen and His word ignored.

There is a verse that says, "No man taketh it to heart.
"Merciful men are taken away," that's God doing His part.
Godly saints will be ushered into a place of peace and rest
while others face the wrath to come, never to be blessed.

There may be more to come, I don't pretend to understand.
But I do trust it will be okay for those held in His hand.
I share my observation to encourage the godly some.
All of God's children will be spared from the wrath to come.

Thoughts on Prayer

God always answers prayer.
Sometimes He says, "No."
He never gets in a hurry.
At times, He seems so slow.

Sometimes He will answer, "Yes."
And He will let you grow.
Yet again He may say, "Stay."
But then, He may just say, "Go."

Prayer is the most powerful thing
that we know down here exists.
We are encouraged to maintain
our own personal prayer lists.

God didn't say we're to go against
the mountains that we face.
He told us to pray and they
will be removed from their place.

God says we are to have faith,
though at times it may waiver,
knowing God will work things out
both in and for our favor.

We need not be panic praying.
We must ask in faith believing.
We'll be blessed in the knowing.
His answer we will be receiving.

Today Jesus Is In The Tomb

Yesterday was 'Good Friday',
He's in the tomb today.
Jesus had given His very life
to wash our sin away.

OH! But watch out tomorrow
because He will rise again
for He has conquered
death and hell and sin.

Such misery and anguish
He had put Himself through
just to offer salvation
to folk like me and you.

So, Resurrection Sunday
is now coming right away.
Tomorrow we will celebrate
that He arose that day.

In the tomb, today He's resting.
Tomorrow He will arise
as He said, 'in three days'.
That will not be a surprise.

Not only will He be arisen.
Soon He'll go back home again.
But He promised to come for us
and take us with Him then.

Tomorrow Is Easter

It is not about the flop-eared bunny
nor the colored eggs that people hide,
it's all about our loving Lord Jesus
and the fact He for us was crucified.

It is about the things He went through,
about what happened to Him that day
when He gave His life for our redemption.
So that we would not have to pay.

We've gone through His day of death.
'Good Friday' though it was not good.
And today we await His resurrection
on tomorrow as He said He would.

"Resurrection day" is what we call it.
'Easter' is its other accepted name.
We will celebrate and give Him honor
being glad that for us He came.

He bled and died a horrible death
so that each of us could forever live.
Tomorrow it all will be remembered
as to Him our worship then we give.

"Easter Day" the churches will be full
of people who want to give Him praise.
Jesus, let each day for us be Easter.
Let us worship You throughout our days.

Trapped In The Web

While walking out in the woods one day,
a spider web was hanging there in my way.
I wouldn't have noticed it 'cept for the glean
shining as bright as any I had ever seen.

I stopped and studied its beauty so rare,
amazed that it was created right there.
The work that must have gone into it
and how each little section perfectly fit.

That big old spider had to be close by
awaiting whatever into this trap did fly.
She would quickly ascend on the entrapped.
Quick as a wink have the morsel enwrapped.

As I stood and pondered this wonder a while,
I thought of how I had seen a similar style
of entrapment, that serves its creator well.
The victim soon falling under his evil spell.

Old Satan is much like the spider I saw.
He puts out his web and makes his draw.
And soon we are doing his unholy will.
He will hold us tight in his grasp until

we see our way out of his trap one day.
We learn that there is a much better way.
We give our heart to the great Creator,
shaking off the web of this intimidator.

Trying To Feel Well

When asked, "How are you feeling?" I often tell
I am doing my best trying to feel well.
Watching the calories of what I am eating,
limiting my intake is often defeating.

This feeling well is a labor of love
taking all my strength in both push and shove.
When I weigh myself, often I have found,
instead of losing, I've gained a pound.

So, I guess being pudgy is now my lot.
It will still fluctuate as likely as not.
Eating more or less, seems I yet gain.
Exercise helps my health maintain.

Sit ups, leg lifts, and jogging in place
are supposed to help me to save face.
But all of these just wear me out.
Making me more hungry, no doubt.

Walking is fine but I have to take a breather.
If people didn't notice, then I wouldn't either.
I can still get around, as you can see.
But this trying to feel well is killing me.

Two Choices

Life gives us each two choices:
stay where we are or move ahead.
We can stay and be miserable
or move forward now instead.

Be disappointed or be glad,
denying the given resource.
Being afraid to move on up.
Sticking to the accepted course.

We can settle where we are
or explore what is out there.
We can be passive and just sit,
acting like we do not care.

When we are deep in a hole.
We can dig or just relax.
Life is going to pass us by
no matter what be the facts.

To stay or get up and go.
Those are choices we're given.
But we can't make up our mind.
We know not why we are living.

We can go against the status quo.
We can resist and use our voices
or sit idly by being undecided
when life gives us two choices.

Unless And Until

People have told me in the past
that something just cannot be done,
and even if you were to do that,
it surely would not be any fun.

But when I hear it is impossible,
I have to at least give it a try.
If it proves out they were right,
you'll hear my discontented sigh.

Other times they will say 'unless'
you can do much better than I
and 'until' that is accomplished,
like me, you will just wonder why.

There are a few things that I want.
There are some things I really need.
But unless and until I try for them,
I know that I will not succeed.

When it comes to knowing Jesus,
I would like for all to trust in Him.
But unless and until they want it, too,
nothing will change for any of them.

Unless and until this change happens,
people will yet remain in their sin.
For those sins they'll have to answer,
unless and until they ask Him in.

Value Is To Be Learned

When things seem to be of no value,
they soon get discarded by the way
with no thought of ever being useful.
They will not ever come into play.

Maybe we did not work for that item.
It was given to us by a friend.
We have no investment in it.
So, on the trash heap it will end.

Value speaks of something precious
maybe referring to its cost.
And we would then be saddened
if it were thus to end up lost.

Value can be found in other people.
The close friends that we have earned.
Or it could be that special lesson,
something of value we have learned.

We must learn to value every treasure
from the bottom rung to the top.
Once we carry our own water,
we'll learn the value of every drop.

Varying Issues

Different people do different things
for various reasons I am told.
It may not be the same thing twice
due to various issues that unfold.

One time, it will be straight ahead.
The next it may be circumventing.
Do not expect any sorrow shown.
Next time they will be repenting.

You can't understand their reasoning
and when you make an inquiry,
they say that it happened that way
because all issues tend to vary.

I must confess that I'm confused
about what their motive just may be.
They shrug and say it is because
various issues are handled differently.

It is easy to get frustrated at them
causing you to bring out the tissues.
They seem not to worry or be bothered.
They're comfy with their varying issues.

Very Soon It Will Tell On You

You cannot hide your sense of well doing.
You cannot fool or trick people for long.
They will see it and know how you are
by whatever you are doing that's wrong.

They see how you act around others.
They see how you care or don't care.
If you acknowledge them as a person,
showing excitement in their being there.

You can ignore all that is around you
and pretend you do not even see.
Or you can smile and extend a hand
and accept them ever so gladly.

People look for other people to show
that they are well thought of, also.
You can fool them for a short while.
Soon they yet will tend to know.

You can be a recluse and stay away
or you can be involved and gregarious.
People just want to be included,
not left all alone and precarious.

If you are truly a people person,
accepting and giving in all you do,
people will take you into their circle
because very soon, it will tell on you.

Walk Away

The New Year is now upon us fast.
There are some things that need be cast
aside never to again come into play.
Just throw them down and walk away.

Walk away from trying to please
people who have you on your knees.
Stand up tall and resist and say,
"I've had enough." Then walk away.

Walk away from bad situations.
Put into place your limitations.
If no value your presence brings,
then walk away from all those things.

There is so much bad going on out there
done by people who do not even care.
Releasing yourself from their control
will be much better for your soul,
if you just walk away!!!

Wall To Wall

When the sun is shining wall to wall
and the weather is warm outside,
it makes me want to be more active
and enjoy what God does provide.

It is a 'Goldilocks' day for sure,
not too hot nor cold, just right.
When the sun is wall to wall,
that gives me so much delight.

I can go forth and get things done
if only I have the mind to.
This is a glorious day for sure.
I can always find something to do.

It's too early to cut the grass.
It hasn't yet grown tall enough.
But being busy while I'm enjoying
can still yet be a little bit tough.

So, I need to stop messing around
and get busy doing some, if not all.
I greatly love this kind of weather,
when the sun is shining wall to wall.

Warmer Days Are Coming

We have had a chilly winter and we now see
the days have gotten much warmer as of late.
We can be outside now on more days than not
bringing to us good things to which we can relate.

The rain is now coming much more often
and it pushes up the soft dirt with each stem.
Soon they will take on their various buds.
Then flowers will pop out on each of them.

Easter lilies and daffodils seem to come out first
reminding us that spring is just days behind.
The time will change, and the days get longer,
an extra hour or so we will not mind.

Shedding the jacket and the coat comes next.
We venture outside the house bare armed.
We welcome the sun and its brightness
and enjoy the way we are by it warmed.

The cold has its own purpose, I am sure.
But when the weather warms, I like it best.
The old bones seem to work much better.
It's by those days we are so truly blessed.

So let us smile and be happy with the weather.
Gone is the bitter cold that was numbing.
The laziness that had settled in is now gone.
We're up and out, cause warmer days are coming.

Wash Day Once Again

You could tell it was wash day at our place,
everything took on its very own pace.
There was water to be drawn for the ringer.
Mom filled the washtub with what we'd bring her.

That old ringer washtub was filled to the top.
Once the washing started, Mom did not stop.
On the old wood stove, water was heated.
After using that, then it was often repeated.

Clothes were divided into colored and white.
Mom made sure they were all washed right.
We knew on wash day, it would take a while
for her to sort through that big, huge pile.

There was no dryer, we would use the sun
and leave them hanging until they were done.
Wiping the clothesline clean was a must,
with a wet rag removing the dirt and the dust.

Soon there'd be clothes hanging of all sort.
A pole in the middle of the line for support.
Towels and shirts were hung on the outside.
The unmentionables inner so they could hide.

Even in cold weather was the same routine.
As you came by, hanging clothes were seen.
Having clean clothes was a necessary thing
regardless of how much work that would bring.

We've Been Trying to Reach You (Please Respond)

I do not think I am important
but they certainly think I am.
Each day they send me bunches
of unwanted, unneeded spam.

"We've been trying to reach you."
Then they beg me, "Please respond."
It's for sure they are persistent
going the extra mile and beyond.

"We have a reward just for you."
Hoping that promise will be enticing.
Their conscience does not bother them.
Lying to an old man is not a nice thing.

They think I'm gullible and will react
but I am on to their every trick.
Spam goes into their own file and then
I delete them with one little click.

It's hard to believe they're paid for that.
Why is it that to them I'm so fond?
Are you also one of their favorite people?
Have they been trying to reach you? Please respond.

What Do You Do?

There have been a number of times
when people ask, "What do you do?"
It seems that they just want to know
so they can better identify with you.

Or maybe they feel over inflated
and they want to prove their worth.
They want to feel more important
than what you do upon the earth.

Or it could be they are just curious
wanting to know what they've missed.
Thinking the grass may be greener
so "What do you do?" they insist.

You smile saying you're glad they asked
because you are so proud to share
and the answer that you give them
shows to them you genuinely care.

You say, "I rush into the burning building
when those inside are rushing out.
I go forth to face the red, hot monster
as I'm trying to save all those about."

"What I do makes a huge difference.
My job allows people to depend.
To them, a firefighter is often critical.
That's what I do for you, friend."

What If I Told You?

Do you have a habit of
believing what you are told?
Do you think that someone
would ever be so bold?

As to blow smoke on you
telling something not true
just to get your reaction
to what they are telling you?

When you finally found out,
would you then be mad?
To know they had fooled you
and you had been had?

Would you show your anger
or just let the thing go?
Would you be a patient person
and not cause anyone woe?

Would you shun them because
they had told you a lie?
Would you care enough to ask
them the reason as to why?

What if I told you
that is what people oft do?
What if I told you that
you sometimes do that too?

What More...Could We Ask For?

God has loved us forever in the past.
He showers us with concern even now.
He promises us His presence evermore.
What more could we ask for anyhow?

He prepares for us a glorious home
and will Himself come for us He has said.
Though we face the vicissitudes of life,
we know our eternal home is just ahead.

He will present us faultless before God
though we sense we've been a failure here.
In His presence, there will be exceeding joy.
All shortcomings and our faults will disappear.

The Savior is now praying on our behalf.
Our infirmities and security causes need.
And even now and for each on our behalf,
He chooses to pray for us and intercede.

He prays in intercession and in advocacy.
He prayed for us here and now we find
though our Savior is now absent from us,
we are yet very much still on His mind.

Christ's prayer will never go unanswered.
We will be safe and secure for evermore
with such love and personal attention.
Ask yourself, "What more could we ask for?"

Elvis "Raz" Stephens

When Life Gives You Patches (Make a quilt)

This saying was posted on Mommy's wall
and it hung there for a long, long while,
each time I saw it and I read it,
I could not help but give a smile.

My Mommy thought this was her life
played out in what the few words said.
She always made the best of things.
I read it again now and I nod my head.

I think there is value in the scraps
if they are put to proper use.
Once they're fitted and sewn together
instead of laying around all loose.

Yes, life gives us each our options
of what we can become and do.
And we can call those our patches
when formly fit we become new.

Making a quilt requires much action.
Being busy with the cutting and sewing
until the patches are sewn together,
there's no telling where we're going.

This saying's much more than cuteness.
Patches into quilts is what she did.
This was my Mommy in all her doings.
There is a quilt in each of her kids.

When Possessions Possess You

In this old world, we must confess
there are many things which we possess.
Yet we are so miserable and thus,
it is when our possessions possess us.

We pile them up and are satisfied
allowing ourselves not to be denied.
Got to have one of most all things
and the happiness that each brings.

Knowing other people are just as we,
wanting something they happen to see.
They don't need it but want it bad.
Just having it makes them feel glad.

What does it do? I'm not real sure.
But I still want it, there is no cure.
If I don't have one, I may need it.
So, I will obtain it in just a little bit.

Too many things gathered after a while.
I don't really know what's in my pile.
But they have a draw I can't deny.
All these possessions, I don't know why.

I think and ponder, "What will I do?"
Some of these things are still brand new.
The answer is as plain as it can be,
my possessions are now possessing me.

Elvis "Raz" Stephens

When Technology Came

Way back yonder when I was a kid,
we went outside for most things we did.
We could find things of interest to do.
Nothing ever got old it all seemed new.

We would stay outside and play all day.
Happy as could be, nothing got in the way.
Everyone knew everyone else's name.
We would play each other's favorite game.

Some were very simple, some very hard,
no one complained about being tired.
We'd run and jump and climb a tree.
Those times were a true joy for me.

One day our numbers started to decline.
Some stayed inside to get online.
I thought that was a temporary kink.
They'd be back out quick as a wink.

But pretty soon, our play had changed.
Play time was forever rearranged.
Our number lessened and then dwindled
as the interest in technology kindled.

So, we're now inside and there we sit,
getting fatter each day and more unfit.
We lost our interest for any outside game.
Oh, the dreadful day when technology came.

When You Pray

The Devil doesn't care about how well you sing
or the volume you use when you give a shout.
But he's terrified when he sees you begin to pray.
He would prefer that you leave that part out.

When you bow your knee and begin to pray,
he will disrupt you quickly if he can at all.
From out of the blue, the phone will ring
with some telemarketer giving you a call.

When you pray, beginning to give God praise,
thanking Him for all the goodness He gives.
He enjoys hearing from you again today.
He accepts your prayers and from all who lives.

You are not telling Him things He doesn't know.
He is all-knowing and listening for you
to come to Him yet again to openly share.
He listens with care as you share what you do.

God has a record book and your name is there.
In the recordings you receive every benefit.
All things done whether large or so small,
they are recorded and listed there in it.

When you pray, make sure to do more than ask.
If you are doing for Him, He'll help with each task.
He will give you clear thinking of what to say.
He is most happy with you when you pray.

Who Is Your Giant?

The giant gave a challenge to God's army, "COME FIGHT!"
Choose you a champion, one with great might.
Let him come against me in a "winner take all".
There was not one amongst them fit to answer his call.

Are you one of God's Champions?
Or are you greatly dismayed?
Who is your personal giant?
Of what are you afraid?

When your giant comes against you, do you tremble with fear?
Can you call on your Savior and find Him real near?
When the challenge is given, can you rise to the cause?
Or does your giant give you many reasons to pause?

Does fear rule your actions?
Someone else runs your life?
Do you have your own giant
that causes you much strife?

Why Didn't I?

Once I created a colored picture
and then began to think,
Why didn't I use more colors
Instead of so much pink?

I once bought a new vehicle.
It was a nice car painted red.
Soon I asked myself this question,
"Why didn't I get a truck instead?"

All through life that happened,
I questioned my decisions made.
Why didn't I do it differently?
Was it because I was afraid?

Now I am a much older person.
Most of my life has passed me by.
Much could've been accomplished
instead of now just asking, "Why?"

I passed on my opportunity
to be saved and on Him rely.
I just shake my head and wonder
and ask myself, "Why didn't I?"

Now the judgment is upon me.
I'm being cast into the lake of fire.
He would have saved me immediately
if salvation was my desire.

I'll live on forever in torment wondering *WHY DIDN'T I?*

155

Why We Read

Do you ever find yourself looking for something to read?
Would you say that reading is something you love to do?
Can you just sit and take up a book you have selected
and in peace and quiet begin to read it right through?

Do you have a favorite author that you follow each book?
They write it so you have to have it as soon as you can.
You already anticipate how good the new one will be.
Getting yourself a copy is now first in your plan.

You love to tell others what you are reading today.
How many books you are into and have on hand.
You smile as you tell them with great satisfaction
because you know as readers, they will understand.

Reading about the life of someone so different
in some other place and so very far away.
The excitement and experiences they go through
just may make you want to go there one day.

We are each made up of the same three things.
Each one is something that we very much need.
The experiences of life, the people we meet,
and, of course, the many books that we read.

Reading will carry us away from the daily humdrum
giving us reason to think and to contemplate.
It will bring to us knowledge of great value
if on our daily reading, we try to concentrate.

Elvis "Raz" Stephens

Why Worry So Much?

Here it is another Thanksgiving Day
and some kin folk are coming our way.
I must get ready and have things done.
A dirty house will surely not be any fun.

What part of the house will they go into?
The bathroom must be shined like new.
The floors must be vacuumed extra clean.
No dirt left visible enough to be seen.

The couches and chairs must be wiped again.
No telling which one they'll be sitting in.
The air must have a wonderful smell.
I'll spray it again hoping all goes well.

Every little thing must be in its place
because I do not want to lose face.
So tidy is as tidy does or so some say.
I'm glad that Thanksgiving is only one day.

I just may be missing the entire point.
Worrying about the impression I want.
Maybe Thanksgiving's more precious and sweet.
Why worry about where to sit and what to eat?

So come on folks and let's have a great day.
I am going to put all of my worries away.
If I'm not careful, I'll lose the Thanksgiving touch
by worrying about Thanksgiving too much.

You Don't Understand My Struggle

"You don't understand my struggle."
I just read that saying in a verse.
That is not to say that I don't care
nor does it mean mine less or worse.

What that says to me is that I need
to slow way down and maybe pause
to listen and make sure I hear you
so I can identify with your cause.

We each have troubles that linger
and will not so easily go away
and it helps if someone will listen
to how we feel and what we say.

Taking both empathy and sympathy,
maybe time you will have to juggle.
It just may require a lot from you
if you want to understand my struggle.

To have a friend you must be a friend.
We have heard that o'er and o'er.
But if we don't notice friends are struggling,
ee haven't taken the time before.

To be understanding, I am trying harder.
To be observant to other peoples' need.
And if I don't understand their struggle,
my prayer is that God will intercede.

About The Author

I try to find time each day to sit at my desk and write poems. Some are very religious and some are thought provoking and some are just out right humorous.

Being retired gives me that time and I fill it by writing poems and songs. I have four children's books, three religious books, and will now have four mostly humorous poems.

I have retired four times and still want to write to fill my time. Please try my books and see if you agree with me that I am on the right pathway.

Elvis "Raz" Stephens

Other Books By The Author

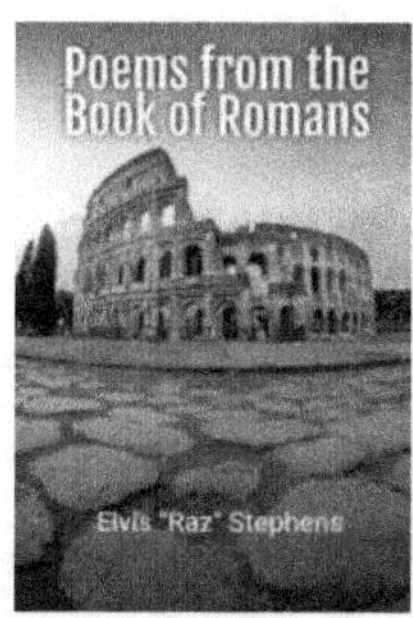